REIKI,
A Way of Life

"After reading this book, I feel as if I've been meditating deeply! What a treat for mind, body and soul!"

Polly Palmer
Reiki II practitioner

"Patricia's message in her book is guiding us to manifest peace, healing and positive changes—not only in ourselves, but in our world. As we heal ourselves and others we heal the earth. Patricia's sincerity and devotion in her healing work and life makes this statement—We do make a difference.

Dr. Dorothe J. Blackmere
author of *Developing Spiritually*

"Travel with Patricia Rose Upczak along the path to enlightenment through Reiki. This book guides the Reiki practitioner through the steps of their personal transformation."

Diane Grandstrom RN, BSN, CCR
Reiki Practitioner
owner of AromaTherapy Plus

"Reiki, A Way of Life" gives one a wonderful insight into ourselves as spiritual and energetic beings. The doors that this book opens are expansive and inspiring."

Suzanne Migone
Reiki II Practitioner

"Patricia Upczak's Reiki book embodies the principal that recognizes that the essence of life is the balancing and harmonizing of body, mind and spirit."

Carol Ameilia Gasser
Reiki Practitioner

"As a student and seeker Patricia lovingly showed me how Reiki could open the eyes of my life. As a practitioner, on my own, her teachings have enabled me to pass on the wondrous ancient healings I touch."

Deborah Gershon
Reiki II Practitioner

REIKI,
A Way of Life

Patricia Rose Upczak

Synchronicity Publishing
Nederland, Colorado
http://www.csd.net/~synchron

Published in the United States of America
by Synchronicity Publishing,
P.O. Box 927, Nederland, Co 80466

Grateful acknowledgement is made to the
Foundation for Inner Peace for permission
to reprint excerpts from A Course In Miracles,
P.O. Box 615, Tiburon, California 94920-0615.
Copyright 1975.

Cover design by Gloria Brown

Interior artwork by Chad Harring and Emily Rose Upczak
Photography by Anne Elizabeth Upczak Garcia

Edited by Dr. Polly Palmer and Anne Elizabeth Upczak Garcia

Printed by Johnson Printing

ISBN # 1-891554-18-2

This book is dedicated to my wonderful, Irish grandmother Rose Ursula, and my two beautiful daughters Emily Rose and Anne Elizabeth.

Preface

Welcome to the world of Reiki! This book is a gift to you from Reiki Master Patricia Rose Upczak, meant to renew, relax, and remind you of the comforting aspects of Reiki and its principles.

Sometimes, after the initial flush of enthusiasm we may feel after our attunement by a Reiki master, and the wonderful group support from our companions in the class, we naturally may start to forget those very principles which not only underlie Reiki, but help to remind us that we, too, are precious and need to nourish ourselves as part of the Reiki process.

I first was introduced to Reiki by a wonderful friend who had taken a Reiki class as part of her Guided Imagery in Music (GIM) course of study. She needed to work on someone as practice, and I willingly volunteered.

My reaction was to fall deeply asleep, not even remembering when I was asked to turn over! Hmm, I thought later, this is interesting. I like this Reiki! My friend practiced on many other friends and clients, and soon we had enough interested persons for a Reiki class of our own, taught by Reiki Master Linda Keiser.

There was something extremely important about being part of this class—so significant that I left a wonderful summer job in Washington, D.C. a month early, just so I could be at that class. Although nothing dramatic happened, the subtle changes which began there seemed to radiate outward like ripples from a pebble tossed in a lake, and I found that people were showing up everywhere who needed to be "Reikied." One of those persons was Pat, and as she tells it, I would notice that her shoulders were tense, or that she had a harried look on her face and simply put my hands on her—then gently suggest that the next time Linda came into town, Pat should consider taking the Reiki class.

And Pat would oh-so-firmly remind me that she didn't do that sort of thing, and she wasn't interested—until one day, when all of a sudden, something **clicked**, and she decided to take the class. She and I are both teachers at a large suburban school, I an English teacher, and she Special Education. I had come by her room to check on the progress of one of my students and noticed an extremely hyper, very tall, very large student romping around the room, obviously on the edge of being out of control.

The student said he would prove that Reiki wouldn't help, and I put my hands on his adrenals while he rested his head on the desk. Bingo! Within ten minutes he was sound asleep and stayed that way for the rest of the period.

But the most dramatic demonstration of the power of Reiki for Pat came, not with a person, but with her wonderful companion, her dog Monty. The veterinarian was very worried because he was close to death after a car hit him. Pat had asked me to "long-distance-Reiki" Monty from my home, which I did. Within thirty minutes of my "sending," Monty got up, acted pain free, and went on to live many quality years. I didn't have to say anything. Pat signed up for the very next class.

My experiences with Reiki have been as varied as any. I once worked on a student's arm through a cast and she healed in four weeks rather than the six projected by her doctor. I have relieved growing pains, stomach aches, and headaches for my daughter, muscle aches and digestive problems for my husband, and neck tension for my office mate. Perhaps the most dramatic indication that Reiki is a powerful force for good was demonstrated for me when I asked my original Reiki practitioner to "send" to my mother-in-law in Iran. She was drifting in and out of a coma, and my husband was beside himself with grief and worry. I hadn't taken the level two course yet, but I knew Sheri could long-distance Reiki her. At first, the energy bounced back into Sheri's hands, and she worried that perhaps we were too late. But then she was guided to say, "If the body cannot accept the Reiki, may the soul accept it." Swoosh! The energy went coursing through Sheri's hands as if it were being absorbed at light speed. Yes, my mother-in-law recovered, benefiting from the energy sent from half a world away.

What I really love about Reiki is that it works, no matter whether one believes it will work or not! Reiki energy is a fact of nature, a phenomenon of our universe, and we can view it as such or see it as a manifestation of the divine if we so choose.

Enjoy this book. Indulge yourself in the nourishing fulfillment of the meditations. Feel the friendly comfort which Pat is offering to you, and freely share Reiki whenever the opportunity presents itself.

Polly Palmer, Ph.D.
Niwot, Colorado

Hawayo Takata

The journey that we undertake together
is the exchange of dark for light,
of ignorance for understanding.

A Course in Miracles, p. 264, text

Table of Contents

Acknowledgments

As I look back over my life there are periods of time that were filled with change and transformation. Often I was completely overwhelmed and vulnerable as I tried to navigate the stormy waters of what appeared to be an endless stream of tidal waves in my life. One of those times opened up some wonderful windows of experiences and healing. I bought a copy of A Course In Miracles, and took my first Reiki class. These two steps changed my path forever.

My heartfelt gratitude goes to Julie Bahne for introducing me to the concepts of A Course In Miracles. I would like to acknowledge and express my deepest gratitude to Dr. Polly Palmer for convincing me, despite my stubborn skepticism, to take my first Reiki class at her home many years ago. I would also like to thank her for the beautiful editing job she did on this book.

I would like to to express once again my gratitude to Anne Elizabeth Upczak Garcia for her editing work and photographic additions to this volume. Special thanks goes to Emily Rose Upczak for her beautiful paintings. They add a wonderful touch of her spirit to this whole project. Chad Harring is an amazing artist and once again I want to thank him for all the help he has given me and especially for his drawings that are included in this volume.

With the warmest respect and love I want to thank Dorothe J. Blackmere and Amy Kees for helping me stay on the healing path for all these years. Last but not least I want to thank all of my clients and students for allowing me to grow and heal with each one of you as you Reiki yourselves and others.

Introduction

Reiki has been a transformative, powerful healing tool for me. The mysteries in life are endless. There is so much to learn and discover.

As human beings we can get stuck in the struggles of everyday life. The mundane can wear us down. However, as spiritual beings having a human experience we can look at life from a different perspective. We can learn to live a life of expectedness, as opposed to a life of apprehension or negativity. I have come to believe truly that what we think about creates our life. We are pulled towards our destinies through circumstances and synchronicities. Our job is to pay attention and take action when the timing feels right to us intuitively.

Reiki helps us all become clear channels of energy and light. The main focus of Reiki helps us become aware of and heal the imbalances in ourselves and our lives. One of the greatest challenges for a Reiki practitioner is to learn to view the world with compassion, clarity, and without judgment.

It is my belief that when a person takes their Reiki One class they are taking the first step on a very long, joyful path. Instant enlightenment is not part of most of our paths. It is vital for our complete health to nurture and heal the multidimensional parts of ourselves. The path of Reiki can help all of us do that. Reiki calls us to be authentic, whole human beings filled with integrity, love and light. Living life with integrity in all areas is vital for our total health.

The laws of spirit never call for us to be dishonest, judgmental, or harmful to another being. As Reiki practitioners we need to realize that every thought we have, and every action we take impacts the entire planet. We must learn to focus our attention and "Be Here Now".

Rituals like meditation, Reiki, and prayer empower us to experience the life we seek. This life does hold challenges and heartache , but it also has unbelievable beauty everywhere. It is important to start thinking of yourself as an energy being along with your physical body. It is my belief that a Reiki practitioner's path includes learning to develop peacefulness, unconditional love, gratitude, compassion, and happiness through an act of intention. I believe we live in a friendly, loving, Divine Universe. I also believe that we receive communication from this loving Universe all the time in the form of signs and symbols. Everything is connected. Carl Jung coined the term "synchronicity" to describe meaningful coincidences that conventional notions of time and causality cannot explain. In this book we explore synchronicity as part of the Reiki path. We are on the threshold of a revolution in consciousness and healing. We are all multidimensional, multisensory beings connected to each other at many levels. Travel with me along the winding, curvy road of mystics, saints, and sages. The mysteries that unfold are the foundation of life.

Unless the healer heals himself, he cannot believe
that there is no order of difficulty in miracles.
He has not learned that every mind God created
is equally worthy of being healed because
God created it whole.

A Course in Miracles, p. 82, text

Dr. Mikao Usui

REIKI,
A Way of Life

CHAPTER ONE

Reiki, A Way of Life

We have been told by wise teachers throughout time that we are not human beings having a spiritual experience, rather we are spiritual beings having a human experience. Reiki changed my life. I recently realized that anything I really need to learn I end up teaching. Reiki is not just a class; it is a way of life. It helps us access our spiritual wisdom. Everyone is capable of learning and doing Reiki. Reiki helps us all become clear channels of energy and light. It naturally helps us all heal physically, spiritually, mentally, and emotionally. Our lives are much like huge tapestries that are woven in combination with our souls, our intentions, and God.

In Reiki we are taught to allow the Universal Life Force to pour through every cell of our being, and then into the person we have put our hands on with intention. In the true essence of Reiki we don't focus on the person's pain, illness, or complaint. We sit quietly and let the energy flow through our hands into the person with full confidence that they will receive whatever they need. Some people just feel relaxed.

1

In this fast-paced world that, in itself, is wonderful. Some experience heat, tingling, fleeting emotional waves, and great healing at a variety of levels.

I have been involved in Reiki for years, and yet I am still amazed and awed by the power of a seemingly simple technique. Transformations that occur in people's lives are gentle, but profound. As with everything, there are people who have been compelled to add to the basic Reiki treatments and attunements. It seems that human beings feel that simple things and techniques are not as sophisticated or "good" as the complicated. I have come to a place in my life where I have realized that the simple teachings of Reiki carry profound wisdom passed on throughout the ages that many of us are just rediscovering.

In Reiki, one of the important tasks of the practitioner is to learn to get out of the way when giving a treatment. In our world, control and power are seemingly important; in Reiki learning to become a channel or a straw for Universal Life Force is the most important lesson to learn. We do not take blame or credit for a person's condition. That is not our job. Our job is to put our hands on the person, with their permission, and allow the healing energy to flow through us to wherever it needs to go. There is a knowledge and wisdom in this energy that is beyond our everyday experience. There is knowledge and wisdom in every cell pulsating through the universe. Reiki helps that person, no matter what race, religion, creed, or class heal themselves. We as the practitioner do not need to know how or what needs balancing or fixing. I like this aspect of Reiki in particular because human error is so prevalent, and I love not having the responsibility of fixing things according to my limited perceptions.

Unlike massage and other hands-on techniques, giving a Reiki treatment is beneficial to both the giver and the receiver. As a matter of fact, the more energy the person getting a Reiki treatment needs, the more Reiki benefits the giver experiences.

For me, giving a Reiki treatment or a Reiki class turns an hour or a day into a powerful, peaceful, healing meditation. Some people in today's society have self destructive behavior. It is my belief that self-destructive behavior comes from unresolved pain. Beings in pain seek relief. My classes are full of people who come to learn how to Reiki themselves. It amazes me still to this day that the simple act of going through Reiki attunements, and then Reiking oneself even partially daily can evoke miraculous, awe inspiring changes on every level.

Self destructive people start to unravel their story and heal their lives. As with anything, this relief varies tremendously. People in pain might try to numb their lives with drugs or alcohol. Or they have some obsession, habit, or object that they focus on so they don't have to deal with or feel the gnawing pain within them seeking healing.

The focus of Reiki helps all of us become aware of and heal the imbalances in ourselves and our lives. It has been my experience that this is an ongoing process that lasts our entire lifetime if we are open to growth and transformation on a cellular level.

The primal energy or life force that permeates all living things is what Reiki practitioners call Universal Life Force. This force has been called many names throughout time. The Greeks called it *pneuma*. The Polynesians called it *mana*. In Hebrew this energy is called *ruah* which means breath of life. The ancient Egyptians referred to *Ka* as a energy force that infused all living things. It has also been called *prana*, *ki* and *chi*. Some call this powerful energy the cosmic breath or the vital principle. All the descriptions cover a force that is the essence of the Universe, of time and space, and is the force of healing, change, and transformation. This force has the power of miracles and creation on all levels.

Some have suggested that in order to visualize this force we could imagine a divine ocean that is an enormous source of loving power. Then picture you and me as tiny drops in this ocean. The power of each drop is part of that great ocean of power. So we are all divine sparks more or less. Reiki reconnects us to our true selves and essence. Reiki is natural for us because we are part of the One. We are intimately connected to each other and everything that exists.

We all have access to that powerful, divine, healing energy. It doesn't matter who we are, what religion we believe in, what race or culture we come from. Those distinctions are not divine, but limited divisions that some people place great stock in. Our vision is narrow. Reality is beyond comprehension. It may be that our journey is to discover the reality of God and our Universe. This must include our own spiritual heritage.

Reiki is not a religious belief; it is a healing art. Reiki cannot be learned from a book or a manual. Experience is really the link. Sages throughout time have developed their healing ability through meditation and years of training. Reiki initially is transmitted through attunements in a Reiki One class. This class is meant to be the first step in a lifelong unfolding of your being—physically, spiritually, mentally, and emotionally.

Over the years I have marveled at the many different reactions that occur in people as they go through a Reiki class. Some of the most dramatic responses include people who have physical, spiritual, mental, or emotional pain frozen in their beings. Reiki seems to melt this frozen energy. One of the many reasons I like Reiki is because people never seem to experience more than they can handle at any given moment. The gentle thawing of their being starts with the Reiki class.

But the class is only the beginning of this process. The

ability to heal ourselves at a cellular level is part of our spiritual heritage. it is stored in our DNA. We know how to heal ourselves. We are wise beings filled with power, love, and connectedness.

Sometimes experiences cannot be translated into language. This is the Reiki experience. We humans want the world to be linear and explainable at all times, because then we feel safe and secure. However, the very nature of life is like the nature of the ocean. A vast expanse of energy we call water is filled with constant motion: currents, waves, ripples, and power. Yet at the same time it can be raging against a rocky cliff on the surface, while its depths are quiet and serene.

There are skeptics that scoff at the idea of an intelligent universe that responds to our thoughts and needs; yet evidence has been mounting for thousands of years that this indeed is the TRUTH we have all been seeking. We are connected intimately to a powerful, loving energy that knows, loves, and guides us at all levels. All of us are connected to this loving energy whether we consciously pay attention or not.

The daily challenges of perceiving the world with compassion, clarity, and nonjudgment is the path we are all called to. Religious belief or non belief doesn't matter. Discovering the vast spiritual horizons within ourselves is what counts. Progress cannot be measured in linear forms. Instead we must refuse to be swayed by angry or downtrodden beings, send them unconditional love, and move a step forward on our path. Every step that each individual takes with love moves the whole world closer to light.

Life is not a tragedy or a disaster—it is filled with growth-producing challenges for which we need to say thank you. Learning to be grateful for challenges and hardship is one of the biggest steps we all need to learn.

Our spiritual growth is important. Compassion, love, and

joy become the lesson and the answer all rolled into one. Part of Reiki training, so-to-speak, is learning to discipline one's mind. Controlling our thoughts may be the biggest challenge to overcome for many people. There is an ancient saying, "Energy follows thought; what you think is what you get." In this day and age we have all heard about the power of positive thinking. What has not been stressed is that positive, loving, consistent thoughts not only help us as individuals, but the world. We can change world vibrations through changing our thought patterns. We can learn nonjudgmental attitudes. We can teach nonjudgment by our actions. We can heal each other by thinking loving thoughts. We are all either part of the problem, or part of the solution.

A Course in Miracles tell us that we do not respond to anything directly, but to our interpretation of it. So then our interpretation becomes the justification for the response. That is why analyzing others' motives is hazardous. We can then get caught up in what we think they are really trying to do—be it attacking us, deserting us, or enslaving us. Therefore, the Course reminds us to leave all of that alone and turn it over to the Holy Spirit. "Every loving thought is true. Everything else is an appeal for healing and help, regardless of the form it takes."

As a part of your new Reiki way of life, develop the habit of daily meditation and positive affirmations. This will help you set the tone for your daily life. Mystics and masters throughout the ages have encouraged us to be still and discover the vastness of our true being and the richness of our interior world.

A Reiki practitioner's life becomes a statement to the world. There are ideals or rules to help Reiki practitioners live balanced lives passed on through some traditions. The heritage of Reiki actually seems to be traced back to the Tibetan monks thousands of years ago and brought to the Western world by Hawayo Takata.

The different groups throughout the world arguing over whose Reiki is "right" does not fall in line with the basic essence of Reiki. This book is not about who is right or who is wrong; it is about healing. Our universe is multidimensional. We are multidimensional, multisensory beings. We need to nurture ourselves with music, art, color, dance, nature, ritual, prayer, meditation, and unconditional love.

Perception seems to be a fascinating concept that we need to continue to explore. As Reiki practitioners it is important to develop the eagle's viewpoint. We must learn that we are not able to judge anything from one point of view.

Another area I would like to explore in connection to Reiki is the consciousness of the atom. Mystics have always known that spirit permeated life at a cellular level. Spirit is God. Throughout the ages God has been referred to as "all there is". Imagine for a moment the Divine Body as the very loom and yarn from which the Universal Tapestry is woven. At the subatomic level, matter is a kind of focused mini-energy field. Consciousness vibrates even in this basic unit of energy.

We have given away our natural power to people outside of us. We let society push us into schedules and lifestyles that are not healthy for us physically, spiritually, mentally or emotionally.

Throughout time the Universe continues to communicate through symbols, signs, and synchronicities. We need to learn to ask for these communications and then pay attention to the answers we get. There are as many perspectives as there are people. We are all looking at the same things from different angles with varying degrees of clarity. We are all going wherever we are going together. Every action of kindness raises the whole planet's vibration.

Our minds seem to be filled with endless chatter as we walk through life. There is a saying that has popped out at me for years that I would like to pass on for your consideration. It might be a personal message, but I feel inclined to include it in this book. The message is simple, as most profound statements are—"Be still and know that I am God."

Every cell makes up the whole. Every cell contributes to the whole vibration. Heal yourself and you help the world. "As within so without." is a statement that guides us infallibly to the Truth.

We can learn much from Nature. Water usually flows in and around most obstacles in nature. Stagnant water becomes moldy and is said to give off negative energy. As Reiki practitioners we need to learn to go with the flow of life. Decide what your life goals are and then turn the details over to the Universe. Many of the painful situations we get into occur because we are feeling fearful, guilty, or stagnant. We need to learn to develop our spiritual path, which helps us reach our goals.

There is a Sanskrit saying that caught my complete attention many years ago. I think it describes everything I want to continue to learn and teach.

As the atom so is the Universe.
As the microcosm so is the Macrocosm.
As the human body so is the Cosmic body.
As the human mind so is the Cosmic mind.

Meditation

Throughout my life there have been times when I have become impatient with " how long "it has taken for things I want to fall into place. One of those times I had an amazing "vision" of this huge universe and an arrow pointing at a little dot with a label saying you are here. The following meditation I share with you stems from this experience. I do this whenever I need to get or keep a broader perspective of life when things are seemingly hard.

1. Relax and take a couple of deep breaths down into your belly, exhaling easily and slowly.

2. Imagine your awareness floating up and out of your body. See yourself from above, then imagine yourself a hundred feet in the air, no longer concerned by the problems that seemed so important.

3. Rising faster, see yourself above your entire town or city, then state, then country until you can see the curve of the earth, this beautiful blue and green ball, receding in the vastness of space.

4. Take another deep breath. Allow yourself to experience the amazing solar system receding in the distance as you expand farther out into space, beyond billions of stars in the Milky Way, then farther until all the galaxies, all the star systems merge into a point of light and you see it all from the very edge of creation.

5. Feel the mystery, balance, vastness, and interconnected power of the of the Universe.

From your vantage point, let your mind pierce the
void with its floating specks of matter, and find a small
star system called the Milky Way.

Then find the tiny star that is our sun, surrounded by
a few bits of matter, the planets. And somewhere on
one of those specks of matter on a planet called Earth,
see yourself, thinking, What am I going to do about
my relationships, my job, my hair, my money?

6. Relax and allow yourself to feel the humor that comes
   from seeing the larger view, then come back into your
   body. Retain the memory of the bigger picture, and
   know that in any moment you have the ability to leap
   beyond yourself and see life in perspective. Or as my
   spirit guides frequently tell me—Lighten up!!

A miracle is never lost. It may touch many people you havenot even met, and produce undreamed of changes in situationsof which you are not even aware.

A Course in Miracles, p. 4, text

CHAPTER TWO

Ideals, Rules or Characteristics to Develop

When a person takes a Reiki I class they are taking the first step on a very long path. A Reiki practitioner's life becomes a statement to the world. Whether we like it or not people decide what they think of a certain course or way of life by the people involved in that "group" as it were. Reiki stands for healing. Reiki stands for universal energy. Reiki helps us become balanced spiritually, physically, mentally, and emotionally. What does that look like?

Balance in the physical, spiritual, mental and emotional bodies is an ongoing, lifelong process. Most people take a Reiki class to work on themselves. So one of the first steps is to take care of your body. Drink at least eight glasses of water a day. Eat healthy food that contribute to the nourishment of your body. Keep your colon clean. Do some form of exercise daily. Breathe deeply. Get enough sleep or rest for your system. Meditate daily. It is also important to use discrimination and your inner wisdom around drugs and alcohol.

Our physical, spiritual, mental, and emotional bodies are interconnected. It is vital for your complete health to nurture and heal the multidimensional parts of yourself. Stress in our society has had a profound impact on people, causing disturbances at all levels of their being.

Modern man has become disconnected from Nature. This is a big mistake. The earth and Nature have great healing power and wisdom. Many people in today's world think that taking a walk along the ocean, a lake, or in a park is a luxury they do not have time for. As Reiki practitioners I would suggest we cannot afford to be disconnected from the earth and nature.

It is important to develop your own goals and become clear on your life purpose. Think through and examine your values and strive to live by them. No matter what your upbringing, release anger from your system. Develop an attitude of forgiveness, not only towards others but also towards yourself. Learn to trust the Universe and let go of fear, worry, and guilt.

Sages throughout time have told us to count our blessings or say thank you for all the gifts in our lives. Strive to be consistent in your approach to life, showing gratitude for things you experience. We must develop honesty and use that in all areas of our lives. This should include work, and relationships.

Years ago I was given the ethical principles of Reiki or Rules of Reiki. It was my understanding that incorporating these "rules" into my life would help me be happier and have peace of mind. These rules seem to be consistent with many spiritual laws I have encountered through the years. Weaving these rules into your life will help you along the path of Reiki in a balanced way.

Just for today do not worry.
Just for today do not anger.

Honor your parents, teacher and elders.
Earn your living honestly.
Show gratitude to everything.

These rules seem quite simple on the surface, but in actuality they are quite profound. Most people change dramatically after a Reiki class.

Often these changes are not necessarily physical. Clarity in thinking is enhanced and often practitioners start developing their intuition, sometimes at a rapid rate. Emotional traumas may float up to their conscious minds, and if they continue the practice of daily Reiki they freely release these traumas from their emotional bodies.

The different reactions to a Reiki class can vary tremendously in each individual person. There is no set pattern. Some people cry almost through the whole class, and then thank me as they leave. Some very seriously depressed people have giggled through most of the class and leave stunned because they thought they had forgotten how to laugh. Many overly stressed, tense people relax so much in a Reiki class or after a Reiki treatment they feel lightheaded.

Reiki defies categorization and classification. However, it does require self discipline. It does suggest letting go of all grudges or anger. It does support us to live passionately. Laughing and crying are good for your immune system. It opens us up to a world that is vast and fascinating, a world where the ego is small and weak. Reiki shows us a path to the interdimensionality of the Universe. We are here to heal ourselves, each other, and the earth. We are all connected to each other with an unbreakable bond. Fighting among ourselves is foolish.

There are many paths to enlightenment, but all of them seem to teach the same basic principles. Some of the principles are learning to love unconditionally. Develop the wisdom to forgive everybody including yourself. Learn to do your work and life joyfully and honestly. Be kind to one another. Release judgment, not only of people, but situations that occur. Consistently keep your body free of toxic thoughts, feelings, words, and substances. Mystics and masters throughout time have told us about the power of our thoughts and our words. Look carefully at how positive or negative your attitudes towards life are, and then make whatever adjustments feel right for you.

The Golden Key is the universal law that is connected to *agape*. Agape means unconditional love. This law states quite simply that you sit quietly, visualize your hope, wish, or need. You then turn it over to God or the Higher Source daily. You do not chew on it like a little dog chewing on a bone. You learn to trust that God and the Universe is handling things perfectly right down to the smallest detail. You keep these hopes and wishes to yourself and let Spirit handle it. The results from this technique or spiritual law is wonderful.

To be truly in balance and harmony also means to be filled with integrity in the way we deal not only with our life, but also other people and their lives. To be in balance, we as individuals need to be at peace within ourselves. If we spend time cheating customers or companies, some part of us is not at peace. Nature works in harmony constantly. The Universe moves with precise movement in accord with every action and reaction. In the long run we will be far richer at all levels by earning our living in a clear, honest way. Our lives will be filled with peace, contentment, and joy if we find balance and joy in our work and purpose.

Reiki calls us to be authentic, whole human beings filled with integrity, love and light. Living life with integrity in all areas is vital for our total health. It leads to peace of mind and body. It leads to peace and joy in one's environment. Parents find that their children grow up less confused when their parents live their lives in an honest way. Children do not generally do what their elders tell them to do. They imitate them. They do what their parents or significant adults around them do. It is a rare child that grows up with a loving attitude towards life and the world without someone in their life to help them get there.

Being honest within yourself, whether someone is watching or not, is what being true to yourself is all about. You are here to be the best "you" possible. No one can possibly judge that, not even you. Follow the rules of your society if you feel that they are honest and fit your true being. But do not follow conventional rules if they violate your integrity, human rights, or innermost wisdom concerning what is true or right for you.

The laws of spirit never call for us to be dishonest, judgmental, or harmful to another being. So it is imperative for the world that people, including Reiki practitioners, live their lives honestly because that will affect the entire planet eventually.

We all learn lessons as we go through life. We are all doing the best we can with the information we have at any given moment. Our job is to learn from our experiences, take appropriate action when the time is right, and become as open to the ways of Spirit as possible.

As in Reiki our lives have a natural order. Energy comes in waves, consistently, in what appears to be random patterns. Everything has a time, a place, and a season. The seasons are very pronounced where I live. Nature is in control at 9000 feet. The powerful energy shifts in all the different weather patterns that flow up and over the Rocky Mountains are a constant reminder to me in my own life to allow energy to flow. Wonderful transformations occur when our internal parts work together, and we stop lying to ourselves or deceiving others. The gates of higher energy and inspiration open inside us when we know deep down that we are acting with integrity. Whenever the ends seem to justify the means, we may not always reap obvious external consequences, but we create inner turbulence that we cannot escape no matter where we go.

Synchronistically, it is important to become a clear channel so the voice of Spirit can channel through us at the right time in the right place. Most of us need to produce an income. Why not do something you love! Get rid of the illusion that certain professions are inherently better than others. A job or profession is only better or worse for you depending on your talents and values. Every field of work has people in it who love their jobs and others who are miserable and hate what they do for a living.

There is a rhythm in Reiki. Allow this rhythm to flow into all aspects of your life. We all impact the world on a daily basis. Reiki practitioners should attempt to impact their world with balance, harmony, compassion, tolerance, gentleness, joy, patience, open-mindedness, honesty and unconditional love. Incorporating these attributes into our daily lives enables us to raise not only our own vibrations, but also collectively raise the vibrations of our planet.

Candle Meditation

Take several deep breaths. Light a candle (keep it away from any flammable material.) Center yourself, surround yourself with Divine Love, and gaze into the flame. As you gaze, imagine that the flame is a vacuum cleaner sucking the negative energy out of your energy field. Do this for about three minutes whenever you feel the need to release negativity from yourself.

Another positive technique that is very powerful is to sit in front of a fireplace or campfire and gaze into the flames. Just relax and gaze into the fire, allowing it to burn up any negativity around you. You don't need to stare into the flames, just relax and go within. Our happiness, satisfaction, and understanding even of God will be no deeper than our capacity to know ourselvöes inwardly. A Reiki practitioner must learn to dwell in stillness everyday. Listen to the silence that begs to be heard.

The Holy Spirit is the only Therapist. He makes healing clear in any situation in which He is the Guide. You can only let Him fulfill His function. He needs no help for this. He will tell you exactly what to do to help anyone He sends to you for help, and will speak to him through you if you do not interfere.

A Course in Miracles, p.161, text

CHAPTER THREE

Trust, Tolerance, and Gentleness

Philosophers, mystics and saints have told us through time to keep our attention on the present moment. Try not to focus your attention, and therefore your vast energy, on the past or the future (thereby causing either regret, anger, sorrow, guilt, or fear of the unknown). Learn as a Reiki practitioner to stay on task—stay in the present. Be here now.

Be gentle with yourself. I always caution people taking my Reiki class to drink water, take naps, and pamper themselves if they can. Listen to that small voice within yourself. The natural rhythm of life pulses through the Universe. The waves of energy that pulse and throb through Reiki practitioners of all levels is both profound and simple.

We can learn a great deal from Nature. Watch the rhythm of the ocean waves and tides. Look at the ripples in the lakes, ponds, and streams as they form patterns that are unique yet uniform.

It is too easy for all of us to fall into the lifestyle of worrying, running around being too busy, and not paying attention to what is real. Most of what I feel is "real" can't even be seen in this dimension, and yet we can affect a whole person's day or life just by a smile or a kind word. Think back on how many times a stranger has made you feel good or made you feel bad just by their actions or words towards you. We all have these experiences daily in our lives. Reiki practitioners attempt to live their lives consciously. We can help each other if we try.

Spiritual laws have been given to us throughout the centuries. One of those laws repeated countlessly by wise teachers is balance. Reiki is all about balance and symmetry. Reiki gently permeates our being at every level, helping us, supporting us to move into a balanced state of being in all areas of our lives. For some of us this balancing act could take years. Symmetry physically, spiritually, mentally, and emotionally is our birthright, but we have just forgotten how truly important it is.

It doesn't matter what happens to you, it only matters how you deal with it. Trust, tolerance, gentleness, patience, and persistence are the keys to success. All journeys start with one small step. Be brave enough to take steps, one at a time in life, even if you are not sure where the path seems to be going.

One of the goals passed on to us by Takata is, "Just for today do not worry." The spiritual and metaphysical wisdom of this statement is profound. Trust that the Universe is friendly. Trust that we are part of an orderly Universe. Trust that we are taken care of, no matter how it appears to us.

I believe God is everywhere, in everything, and everybody. Through all major spiritual teachings we are told to trust God. Worry is not helpful, spiritual, or a positive quality to have in our life. Worry stems from fear. Fear stems from a lack of faith in either a friendly, helpful Universe or

Spiritual Being that will help us if we just relax and trust
that everything is happening perfectly. Either there is a
powerful Universal Loving Being guiding us or there isn't.
There is no in between. According to the Desiderata everything is happening just perfectly. I believe this to be true,
and the essence of Reiki is based on trusting the Universal
Life Force in areas of our lives.

Even the wisest human being on this planet only sees a
limited piece of the whole picture of life. Therefore, being
able to judge anything accurately is an absurd concept that
humans created to make themselves feel more secure on
this little blue ball hurling through space.

Don't let worry gnaw away at your being. Worry creates
fear. Worry never solved anything. Worry creates stagna-
tion in our lives—fear of taking action because of the
unknown, or possible dangers or problems that lie in our
future. Learn to deal with today. A positive affirmation to
practice could be, "Just for today I will not worry."

Stay in the present. Most of the unnecessary pain, sorrow, and torture that we all experience is because we are
not in the present moment. Reliving the past is not only
futile, it causes people to focus on and put their energy into
painful losses or hurts. If it is true that energy follows
thought, or what you think is what you get, then focusing
on past hurt and pain only brings more pain and hurt into
the present moment. Let it go. Focus on the moment you
are in. Be here now.

I have found that it is important to let the Universe guide
us. Come to know that there is a perfect wisdom, synchronicity, and time in everything in our lives. Cluttering
our minds with "What if's?" is not only a waste of time, it
slows down our balancing process. It doesn't stop the
process, because eventually we will all get to "where" we are
journeying. One of my favorite quotes from *A Course In
Miracles* is in the very beginning. The introduction states,

This is a Course in Miracles.
It is a required course.
Only the time you take it in is voluntary.
Free will does not mean that you can establish curriculum.
It means only that you can elect what you want to take at a given time.
The course does not aim at teaching the meaning of love, for that is beyond what can be taught. It does aim, however, at removing the blocks to the awareness of love's presence, which is your natural inheritance.
The opposite of love is fear, but love is all encompassing and can have no opposite.
This course can therefore be summed up in this way.
Nothing real can be threatened.
Nothing unreal exists.
Herein lies the peace of God.

We all must learn to take life step by step or one day at a time. Be patient with yourself and others. Let go of the past, and stop being afraid of the future. All of the sages tell us we only have NOW. Be here now, and live in the present moment. Accept the people, situations, events, or circumstances as they happen. Remember that right now is exactly as it should be no matter how it appears, or how we want it to be. Learn to take responsibility for any of your actions that got you to this present moment, and take positive steps to change what you don't like so that you are not in this sit uation again if you don't want to be.

We have been told that every problem or challenge is an opportunity in disguise waiting for our creative approach to its solution. So be creative, ask for help from the Universe, and **listen for the answer**.

If we are all part of the ONE then the spiritual law that states that giving and receiving are the same makes sense. When you give something, no matter how small, to another you start the flow of energy that helps you receive not only from others, but from the Universe as it moves whatever you have given out back to you.

Nowhere in metaphysical or spiritual literature could I find one example of worry healing any problem or situation. When I was a child my Irish grandmother used to tell me a wonderful story. Coincidentally, I have read or heard three or four versions of this story over the last ten years. Because I believe the Universe gives us messages daily, I realized that this story fits in this chapter.

There once was an Irish potato farmer whose pride and joy was his beautiful, strong farm horse. Every day the farmer and the horse plowed his fields, pulled out stumps, or fixed fences. Every day the farmer stopped work at noon, unbuckled the horse's harness, and let the horse graze while he ate his meal under a tree. One day a thunderstorm rumbled across the green Irish hills and startled the horse. He ran off across the hills, and the farmer could not catch him.

Well, his neighbors gathered together in the local pub trying to console the farmer. They were very concerned and said, "Oh, poor ol' Sean!

This is such bad luck. He will never be able to get his fields ready now for planting." As they started to tell him how terrible things looked for him, he just smiled quietly and said, "We will just have to wait and see. We don't have the full story yet." But his friends and neighbors were very worried. They knew this was definitely bad luck.

A month later the potato farmer's horse came back with fifteen beautiful mares. The farmer corralled them all, and his neighbors crowded around saying, "Oh, what good luck!

This is wonderful!" The local pub was filled with tales of what a great thing this was to have happened to good ol' Sean. But the the old farmer just smiled and said, "We will just have to wait and see. We don't have the full story yet." But his neighbors went away talking about how great his luck was.

A few weeks later the old farmers' son was breaking these new high strung horses. One particularly wild mare threw him off so badly that he broke both of his legs. The farmer's neighbors were back shaking their heads at the farmer's terrible luck. Now they were all really worried!

The farmer just smiled and said, "We will just have to wait and see. We don't have the full story yet." Of course, all of his neighbors knew that poor ol' Sean was cracking up from all the stress he had been under. They couldn't imagine what the old farmer was thinking. Nothing good could ever come from his son having two broken legs.

Then the government declared war and sent out a proclamation to all the towns and villages across the countryside. "All able bodied men in the villages and on the farms are called to fight for their country!" Many knew the country was not really in a position to win this war, so they feared that their sons would not return home safely.

All the young men, except the farmer's son because of his broken legs, had to go off to fight and leave their families. Now the neighbors knew this was amazing luck, but the old Irish potato farmer just smiled and said, " We will just have to wait and see. We don't have the full story yet."

I often think about this story when I am tempted to either judge a situation or worry about a problem.

When I lose my perspective a walk in the mountains, or along some body of water like the ocean, a river, or a creek helps me remember the natural order of things. The Universe is not random. The order of cycles in Nature is perfect; we just don't see this perfection because change is upsetting. A hurricane or earthquake rips up the surface, sometimes causing deep cracks in the outer shell of the earth. As human beings we may need an awakening to what is real, and destroying material, surface things does make human beings question and search for answers.

Life is full of ups and downs, or so it appears to us. The whole "Let go Let God" theory of completely turning things over to Spirit has become a way of life for me. It feels like Reiki in action throughout the fabric of my life. Accepting challenges as a positive way to grow as we climb the hills and mountains of life is an important part of our character building. As we learn to surrender our path to a Higher Source we will be amazed at the synchronicity and joy that come into our life daily.

Another rule that Takata gave us says, "Just for today do not anger." As Reiki practitioners we need to allow the calming, soothing waves of Reiki energy to flow through us. This flow of energy will help turn a person's life into a continuous meditation. Reiki is a powerful, yet simple technique to move into a meditative state easily and effortlessly.

Usually anger comes up because of either frustration, hurt, or judgment of a situation or person at a particular moment. A Course In Miracles tell us we have no ability to judge anything, that our perceptions of people, the world, God, and situations are so limited that we need to leave all aspects of judgment to God.

So when a situation comes up that evokes an angry feeling, we should discipline our mind and learn to control our emotions just for today. A Course In Miracles also tells us there is no justifiable anger, because we don't really know what we are looking at. It is suggested that people and situations need to be healed not judged. Often a person's behavior, no matter how it appears, is simply a call for help.

The Universe provides all ranges and choices of experiences for us. I like to compare them to a giant multidimensional movie with surround sound and technicolor for realistic effects. We can choose any channel, any comedy or soap opera we want. The trick is to remember that it is not reality. Reality is constant love and light. Reality is a powerful, unbreakable bond to a supportive loving Universe that we are all part of. Everything else is more or less a figment of our imagination, like a good novel or movie.

Perspective is a fascinating concept. Everything looks different depending on where we are and how we see things. This is true in art, and it is true in life. The Native American saying, "Never judge another until you have walked a mile in their moccasins," has great wisdom in it.

Anger usually comes up when situations are filled with conflict, confusion, lack of communication or miscommunication, control issues, or feelings of powerlessness by individuals or groups. The Course tells us that we do not have the perspective to judge anything or anybody. All religions tell us it's wrong to judge others; we should leave that to God.

I would like to suggest that it is an error in thinking to believe that we can judge. Our vision is so limited, we do not have the breadth of sight to really know what is totally going on at any given moment in time. The Universe is vast beyond our comprehension. Patterns are being woven in every life we encounter. There are no accidental crossings. There are no accidental events. There are intricate, creative encounters monitored by Spirit and Creation. This concept is completely beyond our ability to comprehend.

Many eastern religious traditions teach that although the Universe appears to be composed of multiple objects and beings, in reality one consciousness pervades and supports everything in existence. These traditions also teach that all our suffering arises because we have forgotten our divine nature and are identifying with our "separate self." Believing ourselves to be separate from Spirit, we lose sight of Spirit and identify with the ego. Alienated from nature, other people, and God, we try to fill our emptiness through amassing wealth, securing power, or controlling our relationships.

The answer to this problem is to develop a way of life that allows surrender to a Higher Power in our daily life. Rituals like meditation, Reiki, and prayer empower us to experience the life we seek. No matter what path we follow the initial steps are the same. Purification can be a slow, painful process. Reiki always starts this process, but a person has to choose to continue purifying their physical, spiritual, mental, and emotional beings. This surrender is not a one-time occurrence; it's a long-term process that occurs in stages. There is no timeframe. This process always creates release of toxins from our entire being. These toxins could have built up over years and years of negative energy being held tightly in place by our ego, fear and habits. Anger often comes up after a person's first Reiki class, sometimes without a specific object to focus on. This is just a release of toxic energy that is foreign to who we really are.

I have been involved in Reiki for many years, and my process is ongoing. When I took my Reiki I class I was in pain around many unresolved issues in my life. By the end of the class I felt as if I had been waiting my whole life to take the class. Harmony and balance poured into my being and forced many things out for me to deal with.

Reiki is about balance. So, loving someone unconditionally does not mean taking abuse and calling it love. If you need to remove yourself from a relationship or situation, you can and should do that, but you need to release any anger or bitterness that follows. Allow a vaster perspective to permeate your life. Everyone does what they do—do not try to judge them because we can't. Love them for who they are, and follow your inner guidance for the direction and plan in your own life.

In terms of energy becoming blocked, toxic anger, rage, or the inability to forgive oneself or another person, is the strongest poison to the human body spiritually, mentally, or emotionally that I know of. Experts tell us that depression is often anger turned inwards. It lowers a person's vitality, immune system, and energy level.

The challenge of forgiveness is formidable. Our growth into a higher state of consciousness is the path that ideally all Reiki practitioners are on. Forgiveness is a complex act of consciousness that frees the psyche from the need for vengeance or retribution. Energetically and biologically forgiveness heals. Let go of all angry thoughts. Holding anger in your being hurts you.

Throughout some very difficult times I have had to continually remind myself that I would rather be happy than right. Letting go of being right nips many angry situations in the bud.

Our birthright is joy. If we are filled with anger there is no room for love, joy, or happiness. Pour out the cup of poison—empty yourself—Reiki yourself—allow the music of the Universe to be heard in your ears.

Color and Light Meditation

Sit or lie down in a quiet comfortable place where you will not be disturbed. Close your eyes. Take two or three deep relaxing breaths allowing the air to come into your body easily and effortlessly. Relax as you exhale each breath. Breathe in slowly and hold the breath for a couple of seconds, and then release it.

Beginning at your feet notice your body. Which parts of yourself are tense and tight. Which parts are relaxed? Now visualize a beautiful white, pink, or green light above your head. Feel that light begin to surround your body easily and effortlessly. Feel the warm healing, and tingling energy of the colors flowing everywhere. Allow your body to fill up with the light, and use it to nourish your organs and tissue. Your body absorbs all the light it needs. Every cell of your body is being bathed by the light. You are becoming a glowing being of light.

Slowly start to radiate that light out—completely fill the room you are in. Picture the room filled with warm, beautiful colors and light—healing and protecting you always. When you are ready slowly stretch, and open your eyes feeling relaxed, refreshed and awake.

Miracles honor you because you are lovable. They dispel illusions about yourself and perceive the light in you. They thus atone for your errors by freeing you from your nightmares. By "releasing your mind from the imprisonment of your illusions, they restore your sanity.

A Course In Miracles, p. 3, text

CHAPTER FOUR

Joy, Patience, Nonjudgment and Open-mindedness

Years ago I heard a speaker quote Teilhard de Chardin. This quote sent chills through my body so I have always remembered it.... "Joy is the most infallible sign of the presence of God." Hummingbirds, kittens, puppies, and laughing babies instantly come to mind when I think of the concept of joy.

This life does hold challenges and heartache, but it also has unbelievable beauty everywhere. As Reiki practitioners we must become balanced in our world view. We have much to be joyful about, and most of it doesn't cost a cent. A beautiful sunrise or sunset can fill my whole being with a multitude of pinks and blazing oranges rippling across the azure Colorado sky, and I am instantly reminded of the beauty and joyfulness of the Universe.

Developing an attitude that is nonjudgmental, unconditionally loving, patient and joyful allows us to not only to heal ourselves and others, but also helps heal the world. Oftentimes when I was asked what I wanted to do with Reiki, without thinking, I would respond, "I want to Reiki the whole world." This is still true today.

Mystics and saints throughout history have offered us maps for our transformational journeys. Religions may be different, but the basic concepts seem to be the same. Learning and developing patience, open-mindedness, unconditional love, and nonjudgment opens up a vast world to us of joy, peace, and happiness. These attitudes are multidimensional and mulitculural—long before these words were developed. All Reiki practitioners have heard that Reiki helps us balance ourselves physically, mentally, spiritually, and emotionally. Think about what that means to you... Where are you in that process?

We are all looking at the same things from different angles with varying degrees of clarity. We are all going wherever we are going together. Every action of kindness raises the whole planet's vibration. We have many sayings to help us remember that developing perspective is important before taking actions that might impact others in a negative or harmful way. One of my favorites is, "She can't see the forest for the trees." A visualization to help us move out of our stuck thought patterns is to see ourselves walking along a path in a forest of redwood trees. Allow yourself to pick a tree and look up. Allow your eyes to go all the way to the top of the tree. Then imagine that you see a beautiful eagle soaring over the entire forest. Imagine what that eagle's viewpoint is. Now look at your viewpoint from the floor of the redwood forest. Take a deep breath and allow yourself to take the eagle's point of view in your life....just for today.

There is a wonderful story that I would like to share. We can, as Reiki practitioners, keep this in mind as we all seemingly are looking at the same thing or process. There once were six wise men of India who came upon an elephant. They carefully started to feel its shape, because, alas, they were all blind. The first one felt the tusk and said, "It does appear this marvel of an elephant is much like a spear." The second wise man felt, and sensed the creatures' side. It was tall and very flat. He proclaimed "Oh no, I have concluded that this animal is a wall." The third wise man had reached toward a leg and he said, "It is clear to me what we should all have seen; this creature is like a tree."

The fourth wise man had come upon the trunk which he did seize and shake. He laughed out loud and said, "This so-called elephant is really just a snake." The fifth one felt the creature's ear and ran his fingers over it. He said, "I have the answer, never fear, the elephant is like a fan!" Now the sixth wise man had come upon the tail, and as he blindly did feel the entire length of the tail he proclaimed, "This creature is like a rope." And so, as the story goes, these six blind wise men each argued loud and long. Even though each was partly in the right, they all were wrong.

This story allows us to realize, even if only for the moment, that our perspective of the larger schemes in life can at best be fleeting moments of the truth.

There once was a beautiful woman named Suzanne. She had experienced many tragedies in her life. She also had experienced many joys; she had a good heart and God loved her deeply. One day Suzanne was walking along a very high cliff near the ocean. She slipped and fell off the cliff. She caught hold of a tree that was growing out of the cliff wall. Now, even though Suzanne was a very gifted Reiki practitioner, none of her training helped her now. Suzanne cried out for help. "Help, oh please!

Is there anyone up there who can help me?" Suddenly the clouds parted and God's voice boomed through the skies, "Of course I'll help you my dear Suzanne. You are dearly loved. Just let go and I will save you."

Hanging on tightly to the small tree, Suzanne looked around and down, and said after a pause, "Is there anybody else up there who can help me?" Often we talk about trusting God or the Universe, but it is in critical times when we are tested that we must have faith in a loving Universe. We are surrounded by help all the time. Leaps of faith and believing in a friendly, supportive, loving Universe helps us live our lives joyfully.

Emmet Fox once said, "There is no difficulty that enough love will not conquer.... If only you could love enough you would be the happiest and most powerful being in the world."

Another rule that Takata gave us is, "Honor your teachers, parents, and elders." My understanding of this rule is to honor the wisdom and soul in all human beings regardless of their age or social status. We are all teachers and students to each other. This response is not based on how they treat us, or what they do to us or for us. All of us deserve compassion, respect, and unconditional love. In our fast-paced, materialistic world, truly honoring or showing respect to other human beings no matter what their age, social status, or appearance is alien for many people in today's society.

The reality is that we are all connected. We are all living together on a little blue planet hurling through space. We are all learning lessons, doing the best we can at any given moment. We are all people in progress. If we are here, we aren't perfect yet. Again, releasing judgment and learning forgiveness are key ingredients to living a fulfilling, happy life.

Many people in my classes have come from very difficult circumstances, and much of their anger is connected to their parents or elders. Life is filled with lessons to be learned. Some of our most powerful and loving teachers are the people we choose as our parents. Often, difficult circumstances provide us with the chance to grow, develop, and become who we are meant to be. It really doesn't matter how someone treats us—it only matters how we respond to it. Reiki is about balance physically, spiritually, mentally, and emotionally, so learning to respond to pain and hurt in a healthy way is important for a Reiki practitioner.

Learn to be easy on yourself and others. We are all moving towards enlightenment together. The time it takes doesn't matter. We live in a safe, friendly, loving Universe. Learn to focus your powerful mind and energy on positive, creative, life giving thoughts and solutions. Release the past. Learn to let go of past hurts, anger and pain. By holding on to these thoughts we create pain in our present and future. Let go.

Understand that there is a difference between honoring someone and letting them hurt you. This rule is not about letting anyone abuse, hurt, or impact your life in a negative fashion because they are in the role of teacher, parent, or elder. Send them unconditional love, and if you have to, remove yourself from their influence and control. It is important to do this from a centered, loving, and balanced place. Otherwise you will misunderstand circumstances and situations that are meant for your growth and harbor deep feelings of guilt, anger, depression, and pain.

Reiki is a safe way to nurture ourselves and others. Its gentle healing permeates every cell of a person's being. This gives us a different perspective of the world and all of the interactions in it.

When we continue to Reiki ourselves and the important people in our lives, the gradual healing that takes place over time is profound. Healing requires a Reiki practitioner to take action. It is not a passive event. We human beings are designed to draw on our inner resources, to find the strength to leave behind our outmoded beliefs and behaviors. Part of the journey towards health is to see ourselves and others in new, healthy ways.

It is important to focus your attention on learning to interpret life's challenges symbolically. Find a meaning in them. Ask yourself how they are connected to your health. Pay attention to how you respond to difficulties and challenging people in your life.

Start to think of yourself as an energy being along with your physical body. Your energy being is the transmitter and recorder of all your thoughts and interactions. Remember, what you think about all day has a great impact on your body, mind, and spirit.

When a painful situation comes into your life, set your sights on the lesson rather than the teacher. Some of our teachers can feel harsh and cruel. However, blaming someone outside ourselves for a challenge is not the point of the situation. Ask yourself, what can I learn from this? We are all teachers and students to each other. We do not ever have the ability to judge others, so bless them, and live your own life to the best of your ability. Also realize that there will be times when you just don't understand the lesson or the situation that you are in. Those times require a great deal of faith and trust. Learn to then say and accept, "I just don't understand or see what this lesson is at this time" and let it go.

A Reiki practitioner's task is to move through personal wounds and pain, not stay stuck in "woundedness." Sometimes the process of learning to honor other people in our lives has a few steps to it. Realize as a Reiki practitioner these steps are important. Often patterns are set in families, and these habits or patterns are very hard to break. A person has to be self-disciplined and structured as they learn to retrain their thinking and reactions to a more positive vibration that may feel uncomfortable at first. Negative patterns may cause us pain, but we have lived with these reactions or grown up with these types of reactions, and it is comfortable and "normal" to do things a certain way. Start one step at a time; release unfinished business. Forgive injuries from the past, and make whatever changes you feel are necessary to promote self healing. Talking usually does not heal; taking action does.

As you work through this sometimes long process, remember that mystics have told us for centuries that all circumstances can be changed in a moment. All illness and circumstances can be healed. Spirit is not limited by human time, space, or physical concerns.

We need to be consistent in both thought, speech, and action. When we let fear control our lives we tend to fear and dislike change. If we learn to accept change as positive growth and challenges to overcome, we are happier. Learn to go with the flow of life; it is healthier for us at all levels.

Happiness is an internal personal attitude. Happiness is a choice. Every situation, challenge, and relationship contains some message worth learning. Negative attitudes and energy keep beings stuck in pain. They feel as if they are caught in the quicksand of life. This is a vicious circle of pain, anger, and bitterness. Positive attitudes and energy push us through the problems and heal situations and people powerfully and effectively. All Reiki practitioners can heal themselves, others, and situations if they learn to be consistent in their daily lives.

Waves of thought create electrical patterns on brain wave machines and, possibly, throughout the Universe. A pebble is small, and yet just throwing it into the center of a lake causes ripples that move all the way to the end of the lake eventually. It appears to me that all life follows this law. Universal life force moves through all of us, especially during a Reiki session, in a gentle powerful way. We have just forgotten who we are. This is neither good nor bad; it just is.

We can choose to focus on the apparently negative things that people do, or shift our perceptions. Life is full of wonders that we really can never judge. We just aren't vast enough to see the whole picture. The whole picture may be bigger than fifty million galaxies.

The flow of life is wondrous with all the twists and turns it takes. Everything is energy. Balancing our lives is more than a full time job. If we were all focused on this, no one would have time to judge or hurt other people. We would stop poisoning everything with toxic forms. On an energetic level it doesn't matter if you are dumping physical toxins into the air and water, or toxic feelings, thoughts, and words into our environment. Energy follows thought— what you think and say creates form in the world.

Filling hours, days, and months with moaning, complaining, whining, and negative or judgmental statements creates a miserable life for you. It also affects everyone that you come in contact with.

St. Francis of Assisi used to call everything and everyone brother or sister. He referred to the sun as Brother Sun, and the moon as Sister Moon. He was very close to Nature. He saw the joy in flowers, trees, and animals. He loved the poor, sick, and the homeless. He treated all people as equals who lived, breathed, and died under the same sun and moon as he did. His prayer is a beautiful guiding light for people of all ages, races, and cultures no matter what their belief system.

Lord, Make me an instrument of your peace;
Where there is hatred, let me sow love;
Where there is injury, pardon;
Where there is doubt, faith;
Where there is despair, hope;
Where there is darkness, light;
Where there is sadness, joy.

O Divine Master, Grant that I may not so much
seek to be consoled as to console;
To be understood as to understand;
To be loved as to love.
For it is in giving that we receive,
It is in pardoning that we are pardoned.
It is in dying that we are born to eternal life.

Meditation

Because we are all interconnected, we can change the world simply by changing ourselves. As a Reiki practitioner, practice a quiet, loving meditation as often as you can. Become a center of love and kindness in this moment. The world will have a nucleus of love that it didn't have the moment before.

Center yourself either sitting or lying down quietly. Place your hands on your solar plexus with your fingers together. Breathe deeply. Take several deep breaths. Allow images of kindness and love to flow into you with each breath. Let unconditional love flow through your being, healing all wounds and pain.

Then focus on your loved ones and send them love, peace, and kindness. Then send out love to everyone who needs love and healing.

Relax and breath deeply as the energy flows through you. Get up and go about your day after feeling reenergized, refreshed, and reconnected to your inner world and higher self.

Miracles should inspire gratitude, not awe. You should thank God for what you really are. The children of God are holy and the miracle honors their holiness, which can be hidden but never lost.

A Course In Miracles, p. 3, text

CHAPTER FIVE

Gratitude and Reverence

Albert Einstein said, "There are only two ways to live your life. One is as though nothing is a miracle. The other is as though everything is a miracle." Reverence is a way of being. The path to reverence is through your heart and gratitude. To live a life of reverence and gratitude means that a person is willing to say, "Life is a gift, and I will not destroy it. Life is a gift; I will show my gratitude for it. Life is a gift; I will go through life causing no harm."

Happiness has many different levels and meanings. It depends on where your intention is at this particular moment in your life. For some it is a meal because they are very hungry. For others it is a good night's sleep after weeks of little or no sleep for a variety of reasons. For some it is a drink, a fix, or some addiction to temporarily release them from some unresolved pain or issues in their lives.

A Reiki practitioner's path involves learning to develop peacefulness, love, gratitude, reverence, and happiness through an act of intention. This takes self discipline, self control, and trust. We need to learn to focus on light. We need to plant seeds of gratitude and happiness. We need to nurture those seeds for ourselves and others. Remember whatever energy you put out on a daily basis comes back to you tenfold. Energy follows thought; what you think about all day long is what you get. So think about things that make you happy. Think about all the things you have to be grateful for...and say thank you daily. Let go of judgment. Life is a journey learn to travel joyfully.

Joseph Campbell once said, "We're here to learn to go with joy among the sorrows of the world." Happiness in the Reiki practitioner's way of life includes radiating positive energy. This does not mean radiating positive energy when things are going your way perfectly. It means going within and developing a positive, grateful attitude towards today.

A wise man told a story to his children. He said, "If we want potatoes we need to plant potatoes. If we want strawberries, we need to plant strawberries. If we want love, we need to plant love. If we want understanding, we need to become understanding. If we want to feel appreciated, we need to appreciate others. If we want to feel loved, we need to give love.

When we practitioners understand this principle our emotional dispositions change from neediness to expansiveness, from an energy vacuum to a source of energy, and from a source of sorrow and pain to a beacon of joy.

We need to recognize our connections to all living things. We are one—this statement is found in all great religious and philosophical traditions since the beginning of time. Reiki is based on the theory that all life, human and non-human alike, is composed of and connected by a divine creative loving force. It doesn't matter what you call it. What matters is that you listen and pay attention when it calls. We are all being nudged to recognize that we are woven together in some wonderful web, through which we affect and shape each other's destiny. Our anger is felt by others.

Our passion spreads passion. Our loving acts ripple out infinitely. We are interconnected to the vast circle of life. So what is done to one of us is done to all of us.

Another rule passed on to us from Takata is, "Show gratitude for all living things." As Reiki practitioners we need to practice an attitude of gratitude. Gratitude is an element of love. It could be considered part of love's rainbow. A prayer or thought offered in gratitude is a reminder of the bond of unconditional love that heals all of us.

Emotional, physical, or mental distress or pain can leave us feeling anything but grateful. But to beg God for help in times of trouble without giving thanks for the times of abundance undermines our attempt to walk in balance. As Reiki practitioners we must learn to honor our divine essence in moments of uncertainty. Just as we teach our children to say thank you, we must remind ourselves to practice an attitude of gratitude.

Melody Beattie said, "Gratitude unlocks the fullness of life. It turns what we have into enough, and more. It turns denial into acceptance, chaos to order, confusion to clarity. It can turn a meal into a feast, a house into a home, a stranger into a friend."

Writing daily in your own notebook or journal is a powerful tool to help develop a balanced way of life. I have found that doing this exercise early in the morning works best for me. Label the sections in your notebook: Attunement, Affirmations, Goals, Gratitude (Thank you's) and Listening.

Under the Attunement section you ask for light, pray and contemplate. You attune yourself to your highest good. I include protection prayers and concerns in this section.

In the Affirmations section I have written some of my favorite affirmations and go through them quickly every morning. For example, "Joy is a continuous part of my life." or " I give thanks now for my life of health, wealth, happiness, and perfect self expression."

Then under the section labeled Goals I have that divided up under Long Term Goals and Short Terms Goals. I review and visualize the success of my long term dreams or goals. Then I go through my short term goals and cross them off (and say thank you) when they are accomplished.

The next section is labeled Gratitude. I take a few minutes to feel appreciation and gratitude for what I already have. I keep adding to this list. This section becomes quite full, and I read it everyday. Some examples of my gratitude entries are "Thank you for my beautiful children" or "Thank you for all the help the Universe and all the loving beings in it give me."

The last section of my notebook is labeled Listening. I take time to listen to whatever inner guidance, ideas, or suggestions I might hear. Sometimes they are simple one liners, and at other times I get complex instructions on what to do. A one liner that I hear frequently is, "Be Still and Know that I AM God!" I think quieting the chatter in my mind has been a great challenge for me.

Depending on my schedule I then sit very quietly and do the Loving-Kindness Meditation. This has been a very powerful tool for transformation. I place my hands on my solar plexus, fingers closed and allow the Reiki energy to flow into me easily and effortlessly. I then take a couple of deep breathes and repeat the flowing statements very slowly:

May I be peaceful.
May all beings be peaceful.
(take a deep breath)
May I be happy.
May all beings be happy.
(take a deep breath)
May I be well.
May all beings be well.
(take a deep breath)

May I be safe.
May all beings be safe.
(take a deep breath)
May I be free from suffering.
May all beings be free from suffering.
Then take a deep breath and visualize a loved one,
Surround them with love and protective light.
Send love to the world.
Take a deep breath.
Continue until you feel loving, peaceful, and at one with
the Universe.

This is a wonderful way to start the day. If your schedule just doesn't allow for the time in the morning—try for later in the day or evening. This practice only requires you. You only need a few quiet minutes and the intention to incorporate it into your life.

Another important aspect of our lives that can show gratitude and reverence is music and dance. Cultures all over the world through time have listened to music to feed, soothe, and heal their soul. Sound has powerful energy. Movement to sound in many cultures is considered sacred. The Native American cultures provide a good example of chanting, drumming, and dancing working all together in thanksgiving for great blessings, or when they are asking for something important for their tribes.

In India, Tibet, and throughout the different cultures in the East, chanting and singing mantras are very powerful and transformative. These practices help us incorporate rituals that raise our individual vibrational field to a higher level or octave, which in turn raises the vibrational field of the entire planet.

Reiki is beautiful. A Reiki treatment is a gift both to the person receiving Reiki and the practitioner. We are so lucky to be allowed to help other people in this way.

The Buddha said, "The only way to bring peace to the earth is to learn to make our life peaceful." There was a story told at the Body and Soul conference in San Francisco about a monk and a man both walking to the dining hall for dinner. As the story goes, if you asked the monk what are you doing he would reply, "I am walking." One would notice that he indeed had turned a simple walk into a mindful meditation. He was completely absorbed in walking. So then if you ask the man what are you doing? He would quickly reply, "I am going to the dining hall to have dinner." Interestingly enough, both the monk and the man got to the dining hall at the same time. One peaceful and calm from being completely present in the moment, the other a little frazzled from always thinking ahead of himself and rarely enjoying the moment peacefully.

The nature of gratitude is the complete and full response of the human heart to everything in the Universe. It is an absence of feeling alienated or separate. Gratitude shows us that nothing is to be taken for granted. Gratitude allows us to feel more together and more connected. When your heart is filled with gratitude, it is grateful for everything and cannot focus on what is missing. Master teachers and mystics tell us when your attention is on your scarcity, you are telling the Universal Spirit that you need more and are not grateful for all that you have.

Gratitude is an inner process. It is an attitude of thankfulness even when things do not look the way we want them to. As Reiki practitioners we can learn to cultivate an attitude of gratitude. Practice developing an awareness of yourself as a recipient rather than a victim. Practice a silent expression of gratitude when you start to see your desires manifesting from the universal source. Develop the habit of not only appreciating the people around you, but also make an effort to tell them that you appreciate them. Write thank you notes to people.

One of the hardest concepts for us all to learn and accept is to develop gratitude for our hardships and challenges. Oftentimes we experience pain and suffering which allow us as Reiki practitioners to empathize with others when they are suffering. Life gives exams. Learn to be grateful for those exams rather than critical of them.

The natural extension of being grateful is the development of a generous heart. Developing a generous heart shows a willingness to give of yourself.

Reverence is a natural aspect of a Reiki practitioner's way of life. Reverence is a perception of the soul. A Reiki class starts a process that heals all facets of a person's multidimensional, multisensory being. This includes developing reverence for life at all levels. An attitude of reverence brings forth patience. With reverence, our life experiences become compassionate and caring.

We have guidance all around us, and yet sometimes we forget to listen, or pay attention. The Desiderata was found in the old Saint Paul's Church in Baltimore, Maryland. It was anonymously written, but its wisdom touches my heart. It seems to go along with the rules of Reiki quite well.

Go placidly amid the noise and the haste, and remember what peace there may be in silence.

As far as possible, without surrender, be on good terms with all persons.

Speak your truth quietly and clearly; and listen to others, even to the dull and ignorant; they too have their story.

Avoid loud and aggressive persons; they are vexations to the spirit. If you compare yourself with others, you may become vain or bitter, for always there will be greater and lesser persons than yourself.

Enjoy your achievements as well as your plans.

Keep interested in your own career, however humble; it is a real possession in the changing fortunes of time. Exercise caution in your business affairs, for the world is full of trickery. But let this not blind you to what virtue there is; many persons strive for high ideals, and everywhere life is full of heroism.

Be yourself. Especially do not feign affection. Neither be cynical about love; for in the face of all aridity and disenchantment, it is as perennial as the grass.

Take kindly the counsel of the years, gracefully surrendering the things of youth. Nurture strength of spirit to shield you in sudden misfortune. But do not distress yourself with dark imaginings. Many fears are born of fatigue and loneliness.

Beyond a wholesome discipline, be gentle with yourself. You are a child of the universe no less than the trees and the stars; you have a right to be here. And whether or not it is clear to you, no doubt the universe is unfolding as it should.

Therefore be at peace with God, whatever you conceive Him to be. And whatever your labors and aspirations, in the noisy confusion of life, keep peace with your soul. With all its sham, drudgery and broken dreams, it is still a beautiful world. Be careful. Strive to be happy.

Meditation

Pick a quiet time in a quiet place. Let yourself sit comfortably. Feel your body sitting and feel the gentle movement of your breath. Reflect on all the gifts and blessings that support human life: the rain, the plants of the earth, the warm sunshine. Bring to mind the many human benefactors we all have: the farmers, parents, laborers, healers, postal workers, teachers, doctors, nurses, the whole society around you. As you feel the world around you, be aware of the problems, and needs of the people, animals and environment . Let yourself feel your heart beat as it wishes to contribute, feel the joy that you could feel by offering the unique gift of your service to the world.

Take a deep breath. Imagine yourself five years from now as you would most like to be, having contributed all the things you want to contribute in the most heartfelt way. Ask yourself the following questions, pausing after each one, letting your heart answer you.

What is your greatest source of happiness? What is the thing that you have done that makes you feel the most blessed? What contribution could you make in your world that would give you the most satisfaction? What would you have to do today to start making that contribution? How do you show gratitude daily for all your blessings? How do you show reverence in your daily activities for the life around you?

Take another deep breath. Close your eyes and relax deeply. Take a moment to thank the Universe for whatever you are grateful for. Take another breath. What challenges in your life have helped you grow? Say thank you for one of them now...

Take another deep breath. Open your eyes and look around. Feel your heart. Have a great day, filled with opportunities for joy and happiness.

Remember that the Holy Spirit is the Answer,
not the question.

A Course In Miracles p. 92, text

CHAPTER SIX

Signs, Symbols and Synchronicity

As we raise our vibrations to a higher level we come to a wonderful realization. We are all one. We are all interconnected. We are part of a vast, amazing, friendly, loving Universe. This Universe gives us signs, symbols, and guidances daily. Our job is to pay attention. As healers and Reiki practitioners we need to develop our intuition as part of our path. As we stay on the synchronistic path we are able to live at ever higher states of energy.

The Universe talks to us. We receive messages daily. Usually these messages come in the form of strange coincidences, or repeated signs or symbols either in our dreams or while we are awake. Carl Jung wrote extensively about the unconscious mind. He believed that the unconscious mind had two parts, the personal unconscious and the collective unconscious. The personal unconscious holds the memories of an individual's entire experience, and the collective unconscious seems to hold all of the experiences of the entire human race. He taught that the unconscious mind had layers of information from all humanity's history. He also believed that all human beings shared the collective unconscious and could touch into it at will. Part of his work revealed that certain symbols are seen universally around the world. Anytime someone focuses on a particular sign, he or she is connecting with the force that has been created through the years by others who have used that same symbol. Our higher self, guides, angels and the Universe gently nudge us with signs, symbols and synchronicities. Only you can really interpret what these mean to you.

Years ago when I was struggling to understand what was happening to me I had several profound visions that I didn't understand at all. One of these was a beautiful large chalice within a giant pulsating indigo circle. Years later I learned that this chalice was the symbol of the Holy Grail. For me it meant that a new phase of my life was about to occur, and an ongoing transformation has been happening ever since.

Symbols usually mean different things to different people, so when working with your intuition it's important to trust whatever first comes into your mind. We must learn to trust our hearts. The heart is usually very intuitive. When you are trying to discern what the sign or symbol is trying to tell you, find the feeling or emotion that you associate with the sign.

Messages can come to us through other people, random thoughts, overheard conversations, strong illogical emotions, songs, dreams, printed worlds, radio, television, movies, animals, nature, and coincidences. Because I love animals I believe I receive messages from them frequently. What I mean is that when I see a certain animal in an intense way (right in front of me) or right overhead I know that it is a signal of some sort to pay attention. The owl, for example, has several meanings in different cultures depending on what the owl is doing when a person sees him. In Native American culture animals are very powerful messengers for us—we just have to pay attention.

A good exercise to become more aware of the signs and symbols in your life is to keep a section in your journal for signs or synchronicities. Synchronicity is a term that describes coincidences of a concurrent psychic and physical event that defies the probability of chance and is meaningful. You will be amazed at how they start to add up.

For Dr. Carl Jung the phenomenon of the "meaningful coincidences" was a missing piece to the puzzle of the psyche. Much has been written on the subject since Jung's book was first published. Psychologists, physicists, and other professionals have been searching for an explanation of how synchronicity works. Their theories range from "the acausal connecting principle," "the unifying principle behind meaningful coincidences, individual consciousness, and the totality of space and time", to "the activation of archetypes" and "unconscious compensation" in the psyche.

Our lives are nothing other than the harmonious interaction of all the elements and forces that structure the Cosmos. Our bodies are in constant and dynamic exchange at a cellular level. We are not static, solid forms. We have layers of energy fields that interact with each other constantly.

Life doesn't have to make sense to us all the time. It is possible we really don't understand what is going on most of time. Life not only can appear random, but actually seems to be filled with chaos. However, chaos can be self perpetuated. We can choose another path if we don't like what is going on in our lives at the present time. I often use the words, "I would rather be happy than right." This helps me immensely in my daily life. We must learn to stay in the moment, accepting what is happening at that particular time while keeping positive thoughts about our goals.

Sometimes it is really hard to do this, because the daily soap operas can appear to be real. Know that your dreams will eventually come true if you put them out to the Universe as a request. Know also that we truly don't have or need to have control over what is happening. Trust that God and the Universe has a Divine Intelligence and wisdom that is greater than our conscious minds. Consistently focus on your goals and dreams, and let God handle the details.

Patience and trust are also part of the Reiki life. We trust that the person we are giving Reiki to is getting exactly what they need. We don't have to aim the Reiki or make sure just the right amount of energy goes in—-it just does. Perfectly. I believe the entire Universe is like that. Many of us just haven't become conscious of how our lives could be or really work. We become locked in the material realm and forget the rest of the levels. Everything must flow equally. Energy is not dormant. It moves, flows, interacts with all life in a harmonious, fluid way. There is a connection between the ancient healing art of Reiki and the new paradigm shift in science. There is a bridge of knowledge for all of us in Reiki as a healing art and is a way of life.

We are told by A Course in Miracles that our relationship is with the Universe. This means to me that there is a dynamic interrelationship with everything. We love and interact at a cellular level with everything all the time whether we are conscious of it or not.

Observe the interaction between the Universe and you. We are all connected. Carl Jung coined the term "synchronicity" to describe meaningful coincidences that conventional notions of time and causality cannot explain. Synchronistic experiences point to a profound relationship or interconnection between all parts of the Universe. These experiences surprise and confound the purely rational mind. Most people do not have a framework for "a random happening that seem to fit our needs" beyond coincidences.

We must learn that the universe does provide us with the tools to follow our destiny. In the fall of 1997 I attended the Body & Soul Conference in San Francisco where I heard many wonderful speakers give presentations. One story I heard stood out, and I knew I needed to use it for this book. James Redfield was talking about how important it is to follow synchronistic nudges from the universe. He used a story about Abraham Lincoln (that, about whom, interestingly enough, I have read several accounts of since then.)

As the story goes, an old peddler, who was down on his luck, came to Abraham Lincoln one day with a barrel of goods. The peddler told Lincoln he would sell him the whole barrel for a dollar. He told Lincoln he really needed the dollar even though the contents of the barrel were not of much value. Lincoln, being the kind man that he was, gave the man a dollar for the barrel even though he could not imagine any use that he would have for its contents. Some time later when Lincoln finally got around to clearing out the barrel, he found a complete set of law books at the bottom, (According to Ira Progoff in his book *Jung, Synchronicity and Human Destiny*, these books were Blackstone's Commentaries). It was the synchronistic acquisition of these books that enabled Abraham Lincoln to follow his destiny, become a lawyer, and eventually president.

Joseph Campbell describes the miracle of what he called the "helping hands" phenomenon in his book *The Power of Myth*. The basic concept of this phenomenon is when you ask God for help, all of a sudden people and opportunities show up out of the blue to help you do what you are trying to do.

Synchronicity fascinates me. It fills me with a knowing that somehow the entire Universe is a perfect, orderly place that listens to us. The coincidences, signs, and symbols that crop up in my daily life amaze me. I wonder how many messages I missed in my younger, more chaotic days.

We all go through tests, and because we are basically interacting and vibrating constantly on many levels at the same time, we can sometimes get overwhelmed. Relax. Don't be hard on yourself—take a walk, play with a dog or a kitten, go to a movie or plan a weekend trip somewhere. Trust the Universe. Know that there really is a perfect plan for you, especially when you ask for help. You always get it. It may not occur in your expected framework of time, but in a grander scheme of Cosmic time that actually works out better for everyone involved.

Let yourself enjoy little things like a bird singing or a sunrise. They are so beautiful, and yet many people think they have more important things to do on a daily basis. It is amazing that synchronistic happenings occur all the time, and for the most part go either unnoticed or barely mentioned in passing as weird, strange, or funny. Coincidences are not random. The more we still our minds and let ourselves tune into the vastness of not only the Universe, but our own spiritual depths and awareness, the more we notice and become aware of.

The vibration of the planet is rising. We are becoming more sensitive to everything that happens around us. As a group, human beings are learning more about their rich spiritual history. Information is filtering into every sector of society. Many people are becoming aware of books like *A Course In Miracles*, and *The Celestine Prophecy*. Reiki and many forms of alternative healing are moving into the mainstream.

Larry Dossey says, "Our thoughts are like loaded guns." If energy is everywhere and your thoughts can be transferred across time and space easily, then our thoughts not only impact outcomes, but other peoples' lives. So we must be careful with that power. Self discipline is very important for a Reiki practitioner.

Mundane activities like chopping wood, carrying water, or gardening connect us all to the Divine—especially if we do these activities in Nature. We can learn great lessons from Nature if we are open to being taught. Animals, trees, mountains, rivers, oceans, crystals, flowers, powerful winds and gentle breezes whisper messages to us from the realm of Spirit. Our job is to be receptive to those whisperings and to allow our intuition to grow and develop day by day. Listen and life gives you the answers you seek. It is very important to release judgment even in our daily life because the mysteries of the Universe are orderly and friendly.

I have spent hours of my life at tide pools along the Pacific Ocean. The worlds within the tide pools and powerful teeming ocean are remarkable. Each wave picks up waiting dolphins and sea lions prepared to ride close to the shore. It occurs to me that our lives are much like that. If we are prepared for the next set of waves of opportunity we are helped by the energy of the Universe to move forward. If we are not prepared or we don't want to go the way the powerful ocean wave is going, we have to go against the tide, or up and over the wave. Sometimes there are long stretches in between wave sets while water is seemingly calm and nothing appears to be happening. Then all of a sudden a wave forms as it surges up from the vast deep ocean. Movement is constant within the ocean, but sometimes it is only noticeable to us along the shoreline or during a storm. Learning to notice the signs tell us when a wave is coming. Surfers or sailors can tell you many stories of the temperament and language of the sea.

The purpose of Carl Jung's effort to understand the microcosmic/macrocosmic conception of the universe led him to the analysis of archetypes and is the foundation of his theory of synchronicity. Jung and many of his followers believed that the experience of an archetypal symbol results in a sense of relationship to the interior workings of life, and a definite sense of participation in the movement of the Cosmos. It has been my experience that this happens more often as a Reiki practitioner slowly becomes more balanced in their lives physically, spiritually, mentally, and emotionally. Archetypes are thought to be transcendent and to be a manifestation of the macrocosm in microcosmic form. When we experience a synchronistic occurrence, this serves as a link between the Reiki practitioner and Spirit. It doesn't matter what image Spirit or the Divine takes for this experience to happen. The Universe cares about us and leads us towards our destinies. We can go against the current or waves of opportunities to move forward as long as we want —eventually we grow and change in a positive way. Eternity is a long time and as *A Course In Miracles* tells us we can't establish the curriculum, but we can decide when we want to learn the lesson and move forward.

Through the chaos theory and fractal geometry we see that certain patterns reoccur at different levels. In the flow of fluids these are the same kinds of patterns in a stirred cup of tea, in whirlpools, in tornadoes, and in the global atmospheric systems. There are also spiral patterns in galaxies. The orbits of the planets around the sun are reflected in the atoms, with the nucleus like the sun and the orbiting electrons like the planets. Science is revealing many kinds of microscopic and macroscopic connections and similarities at every level.

Everything in the Universe is connected, vibrating and humming throughout the Cosmos. We are part of those vibrations. Our thoughts and words have impact on that Universe. We send out messages of need, and the Universe sends us signs, symbols, and synchronicities in response to our need.

If we are all connected in the Universe, then it is vital as we develop our role as Reiki practitioners to also develop our compassion. The Dalai Lama said, "There is no need for temples, no need for complicated philosophy. Our own brain, our own heart is our temple; the philosophy is kindness." As healers we must keep in mind the vision of our connection to a vital, loving responsive Universe that we are part of. Black Elk tells us in order to truly be at peace within our hearts and minds we must realize our relationship and oneness with the Universe, "and all its powers, and when we realize that at the center of the Universe dwells Wakan-Tanka, and that this center ... is within each of us..." then peace and healing will flow everywhere.

Throughout time, in all cultures, leaders have taken us to this point in our consciousness. It is time to take another step forward together. Reiki practitioners have the tools to create wholeness in their lives and in the world around them. As individuals and as a group we can help heal each other. It all starts with each individual following his/her own inner guidance, intuition and path to healing. We are multidimensional beings with complex energetic fields. Our etheric body is a holographic energy field that carries information for the growth and repair of the most dense field we have, the physical body.

The Universe seems to be a giant hologram, possibly a Divine hologram. Our paths and destinies intertwine, allowing us to heal and help each other towards joy, happiness, and fulfillment. Signs, symbols, and synchronicities are just messages to pay attention to along the way.

There is a pulse in all things. The pulse of your heartbeat is the most familiar to people. Reiki often gently throbs or pulses through a practitioner's hands as he/she work on another. I like to compare this to the heartbeat of God, the pulse of Universal Life Force that flows through, in, and around everything. We have so many reminders in this day and age to wake up and remember what we are capable of and who we are really. The Universe is vast beyond our comprehension. Patterns are being woven in every life we encounter. There are no accidental crossings. There are no accidental events. There are intricate, creative encounters

monitored by God and Creation. This concept is completely beyond our ability to comprehend.

We all suffer from the delusion of separation. This separation is very painful and lonely. At some level we all know
that there is something better and different from a rat race,
or dog eat dog society where we are all wary of each other.
Fear rules many lives, not just daily, but for years. Guilt creates rules that make no sense other than to control large
groups of people. Creative, sensitive beings become overwhelmed by their pain, killing themselves senselessly. Life
becomes a cheap commodity when in reality life is far more
valuable than any amount of wealth or gold. We need to
shift our priorities in life,to follow a way of life that values
all forms of life no matter what age, color, race, religion or
class. Animals and plants contribute immensely to our
world, and yet many people have become numb with the
technological age. We need to balance our existence with
serenity, peace, love, and nurturing. We need to love each
other unconditionally. We need to change our vibrations to
a higher level without anger and violence.

As Reiki practitioners we need to change the way we
look at situations and experiences. Reiki helps us stretch
our perspective. As we learn to shift the way we perceive
ourselves and others, we develop the intuitive ability to
become aware of the synchronicities in our lives. We need
to learn to listen to the messages the Universe constantly
gives us through signs and symbols.

Clearing and Regenerating Energy Field Meditation

Masters throughout time have given us many techniques for clearing and healing our bodies. This includes our auras and chakras.

Sit or lie down comfortably. Take a deep breath. Relax. Put your hands either loosely at your side or on your solar plexus. Close your eyes and imagine that you are surrounded by deep, rich, red light filling your whole body with energy and power. Let the color wrap around you for several minutes filling your energy field with warmth and vibrant energy.

Take another deep relaxing breath. Imagine a beautiful orange color surrounding your entire being with vibrant, creative energy. Let the color wrap around you, circling your entire body with color for several minutes.

Take another deep breath, relaxing deeply. Imagine a bright, vivid yellow color swirling around you completely. Let that bright, clear, yellow color heal you as it swirls and pulses through every cell in your body and energy field. Let that yellow color fill your entire being with joy, laughter, and power. Allow that yellow to surround you for several minutes.

Take another deep breath. Imagine a beautiful green color wrapping itself around you in a loving beautiful softness. Allow the loving, compassionate, balanced green to fill your energy field with peace and love. Wrap yourself in this serene green for several minutes. Fill your entire being with the unconditional love of your fourth chakra. Allow yourself to feel the peaceful green color softly fill you up.

Take another deep breath. Imagine a brilliant blue color surrounding you easily and effortlessly. Wrap your whole being in this beautiful blue color filled with communication and creativity. Feel the vibrant blue color rippling through your energy field like ocean waves for several minutes. Relax.

Take another deep breath. Imagine a deep indigo color pulsating brilliantly. Wrap your entire body and energy field in this beautiful indigo color for several minutes. Allow your imagination and intuition to open up as this color fills you up for several minutes.

Take another deep, deep breath. Imagine a beautiful purple color swirling around your entire body and through every cell of your body. Feel it pulse through your crown chakra. Feel it beat with every beat of your heart. Feel it fill your entire being with understanding, bliss, and knowledge. Feel its connection to your higher self for several minutes.

Take another deep breath and imagine that your crown chakra becomes like a waterfall of blazing white light that completely surrounds and heals you at all levels. Relax and feel the peace of Universal Love pouring around you and in you. Take another breath. Wiggle your fingers and toes. Slowly stretch and open your eyes. Notice how the colors of nature and your world start looking brighter after doing this meditation for awhile. Do this everyday if you can, and you will feel brighter and lighter. Pretend that this is your daily shower, your shower of colors for your energy field.

All healing is release from the past. That is why the Holy Spirit is the only Healer. He teaches that the past does not exist, a fact which belongs to the sphere of knowledge, and which therefore no one in the world can know. It would indeed be impossible to be in the world with this knowledge. For the mind that knows this unequivocally knows also it dwells in eternity, and utilizes no perception at all. It therefore does not consider where it is, because the concept "where" does not mean anything to it. It knows that it is everywhere, just as it has everything, and forever.

A Course In Miracles, p.240, text

CHAPTER SEVEN

The Consciousness of the Atom

As Reiki practitioners we are on the threshold of a revolution in consciousness and healing. We are all multidimensional beings connected to each other at many levels. Throughout time God has been referred to as "all there is". Imagine the Divine Body as the very loom and yarn from which the Universal Tapestry is woven. Matter, even at the subatomic level is a kind of focused mini-energy field. There is a consciousness in this basic energy unit.

Reiki practitioners feel energy waves flow through their bodies and hands into another person every time they Reiki someone. We know that energy we cannot see without physical eyes exists. When one accepts the premise that every atom possesses a form of consciousness, it is easier to understand that atoms of like vibrational patterns come together to form a specific body of energy.

In nature this is known as the Law of Attraction, where atoms of similar structure or vibration gather together and vibrate in unison, thus producing a physical form or aggregation of atoms.

As the atom so is the Universe
As the microcosm so is the Macrocosm
As the human mind so is the Cosmic Mind.
As the human body so is the Cosmic Body.

This ancient saying taken from the Sanskrit text is the foundation for what Reiki is. Mystics and scientists are investigating the subtle energies of the Universe. These energies are multidimensional and multifaceted. They are beyond our ability to define.

Throughout literature we have read the esoteric truism, "as above, so below," and recognize that the tiny atom is within itself a solar system of expression, differing from other atoms according to the arrangement and number of electrons around the central charge. We can perceive that this theme is being repeated over and over again in countless forms and expressions, and recognize that we are all a part of the One Whole.

Everything pulsates with energy, and all of this energy contains information. Our physical bodies are surrounded by an energy field that extends as far out as your outstretched arms and the full length of your body. This energy field is a highly sensitive perceptual system and information center. Whether we know it or not, we are constantly in communicatiion at some level with everything around us. There is a conscious electricity that transmits and receives messages to and from other people's bodies, and sometimes even places and environments that we walk through.

There are not random happenings. At at cellular level there is loving intelligence. Learn to go with the flow. There is a connection between the ancient healing art of Reiki and the new paradigm shift in the science of the 20th and 21st centuries. There is a bridge of knowledge for all of us in Reiki, both as a healing art, and as a way of life. We are evolving, learning, and growing together.

Reiki heals and balances a person's physical. spiritual, mental and emotional energy bodies of different vibrations. Experiences that carry emotional energy in our energy system can include relationships, traumatic experiences, belief patterns, and attitudes. Apparently the emotions from these experiences become encoded in our biological systems and may contribute to the formulation of our cell tissue, which then generates a quality of energy that reflects those emotions. Consistent Reiki treatments can help a reiki practitioner balance and heal those cells, releasing negative emotional patterns over time. Dr. Candace Pert, a neurobiologist, has shown that neuropeptides (the chemicals triggered by emotions) are thoughts converted into matter. Our emotions interact with our cells and tissues. Dr. Pert also says that the same kinds of cells that manufacture and receive emotional chemistry in the brain are present throughout the body. So all of our cells have intelligence. Your heart intuitively "knows" what is right for you possibly before your conscious mind is aware of what decision to make about a situation.

Thousands of years ago the ancient sages of India and Tibet called the subtlest form of energy *Prana*. *Prana* is present in every mental and physical event; it flows directly from spirit, to bring consciousness and intelligence to every part of life. The more Reiki practitioners Reiki themselves and others, the more *prana* they have vibrating throughout their being.

Quantum physics tells us that there is no end to the cosmic dance—the universal field of energy transforms itself, becoming new every second. Our bodies follow the same pattern. Scientists tell us that there are over six trillion reactions taking place in each cell every second. The skin replaces itself once a month, the stomach lining about every five days, the liver every six weeks, and the bones in your skeleton every three months. We have exchanged 98% of the atoms in our bodies for new ones by the end of a year.

Our energy field has several layers called subtle bodies. As with everything connected to discussions around subtle energies, the vocabulary is not exact. Some terms are used differently by different teachers. The etheric body (called the blueprint field in England) is the shape of the physical body. This layer has also been called the "vital layer or thermal body," and it can be detected with infrared cameras. Second is the emotional body, usually described as the field of emotions and feelings surrounding us. Third is the mental body also known as the causal body, where thoughts, mental processes, and visual imagery are contained. Fourth is the astral body associated with heart and intuition. Fifth is the celestial body. Sixth is the ketheric body. Both of these bodies are associated with spiritual realms and interactions.

It is not important to understand the details of the energy bodies. But it is important to realize that the physical body is encased in these energy bodies. Reiki affects all of a person's seven bodies in a gradual, powerful, gentle way. Oftentimes the most important healing that takes place is in the energy field around the physical body. This protects the physical body from further damage or problems.

For thousands of years Asian conceptions of our energy anatomy from China and India have shared the understanding that there are pathways along which our vital energy flows through our body. In Chinese medicine these pathways are called our meridians and in India they are called our nadis. These pathways form the basis of acupuncture and Asian medicine. Scientists are starting to prove that meridians emit light and can be seen with infrared photography.

There are also major centers of both electromagnetic activity and the pooling and circulation of vital energy. In the Huna tradition of Hawaii they are called AUW centers. In the Cabala they are the tree of life centers. In the yogic theory the term for these centers are called Chakras.

In healing, especially energy healing, there are eleven to fifteen chakras involved.

Chakra	Location	Function	Organs Influenced
Crown	crown of the head		connected to the brain and pineal gland
Forehead	center of forehead		nervous system and pineal gland
Ajna	between eyebrows	controls the other chakras	pituitary gland and endocrine glands
Throat	center of throat	controls	throat, thyroid, and parathyroid glands
Heart			
1) front	center of chest		heart, thymus gland and circulatory system
2) back	back of the heart		lungs and the heart
Solar plexus			
1) front solar plexus	hollow area between ribs	Seems to act as an energy clearinghouse.	Connected to pancreas, liver, large intestine, diaphragm, appendix, stomach, and small intestine
2) back solar plexus	directly opposite the front solar plexus chakra	Controls the temperature of body.	
Spleen			
1) front spleen	left part of the abdomen between the front solar plexus and the navel chakra		spleen
2) back spleen	back of front spleen chakra		
Navel	navel	controls	small and large intestines

Continued on next page

Chakra	Location	Function	Organs Influenced
Meng mein	back of the navel	controls	kidneys, adrenal glands, and blood pressure
Sex chakra	pubic area	controls	sexual organs, bladder and legs
Basic	base of spine	energizes the body and affects general vitality, growth, and body heat.	adrenal glands and sex organs

See charts and drawings for correct placement of these chakras. There are also chakras in the palm of your hands and on your feet.

Energy Fields

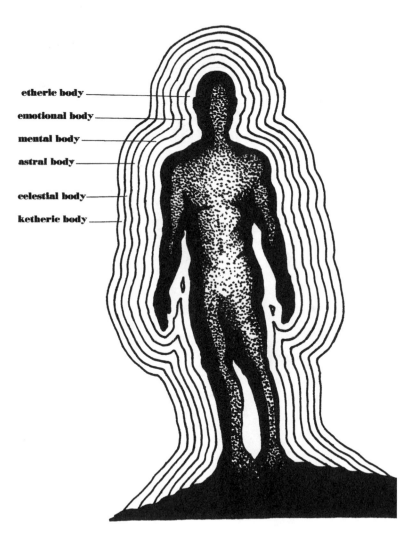

etheric body

emotional body

mental body

astral body

celestial body

ketheric body

Major Chakras on the Front of the Body

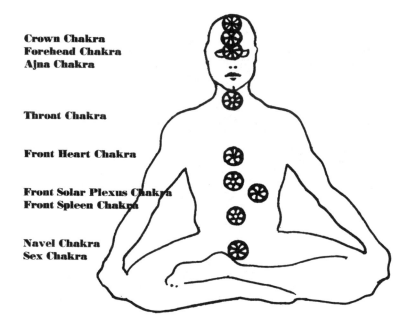

Crown Chakra
Forehead Chakra
Ajna Chakra

Throat Chakra

Front Heart Chakra

Front Solar Plexus Chakra
Front Spleen Chakra

Navel Chakra
Sex Chakra

Major Chakras on the Back of the Body

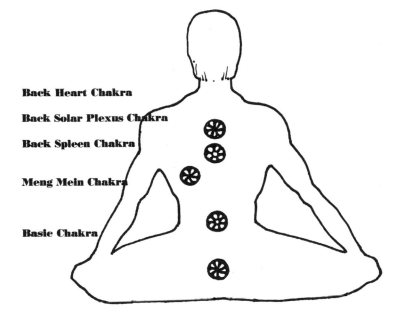

Back Heart Chakra

Back Solar Plexus Chakra

Back Spleen Chakra

Meng Mein Chakra

Basic Chakra

In the ancient texts the seven most prominent chakras also have other traits and colors associated with them. These are as follows:

crown chakra is connected to the color violet and bliss, understanding and knowledge.

ajna chakra is connected to the indigo color and dreaming, imagination, and intuition.

throat chakra is connected to a bright blue color and communication, creativity and connection.

heart chakra is connected to the color green and love, balance, and compassion.

solar plexus chakra is connected to a bright yellow color and power, will, laughter, anger, and joy.

sex chakra is connected to the color orange and to desire, sexuality, and tears.

basic root chakra is connected to a deep red color and survival, grounding, and stillness.

Reiki speeds up the natural order of the healing process that is constantly going on in our being at all levels. The chakras, or whirling energy centers, are a very important part of the human energy field. The chakras are centers of activity for the reception, assimilation, and transmission of life energies. It is our natural state to feel peaceful, healthy, happy, and loving. It appears that our energy fields and centers are even designed to help keep us that way. Reiki supports that design naturally. Reiki inherently dissolves the blocks in our physical, spiritual, mental and emotional bodies.

There is a consciousness in every cell of the body; all we have to do is communicate and honor that consciousness in our everyday lives. If we all did this we could change the world to a healed, balanced planet.

Love is the richness and fullness of our souls flowing through us. Forgiveness, clarity, humbleness, compassion, love, and an attitude of nonjudgment are the dynamics of freedom. They are the foundations of who we really are. As Reiki practitioners we are drawn to walk the path that is our soul's destiny. Until we fulfill that destiny we will be seekers, looking for the truth and fulfillment that our souls yearn for. Material things and objects can not satisfy that hunger. Our spiritual need to grow in love, joy, and compassion is ingrained in us right down to the smallest atom in our being.

If we realize only for a moment that there is a pulsating, vibrating consciousness in every atom, then we have to change our world view. As Reiki practitioners we are taught that there is an energy field around everything. Now we are being taught that energy has consciousness; a unique vibration humming brilliantly for those who can hear its music. We need to allow ourselves to be open to the many layers of energy and dimensions around us. The Universe is ours to explore and appreciate. It seems to be waiting, patiently, for us to glimpse reality through the curtains of shadowy illusion. With each step of awareness arenas of information are opened up for our investigation. As we come to understand what we see, feel, and channel as Reiki practitioners we can help the rest of the world more on a daily basis. Understanding permeates the collective consciousness raising the vibration of the whole. I believe that is an important part of the path of a Reiki practitioners life.

James Redfield once said, "Do not leave the house until you can put yourself in a positive, spiritual frame of mind." As human beings we can get stuck in the struggles of everyday life. As spiritual beings having a human experiences we can look at life from a different perspective. We are pulled

towards our destinies through circumstances and synchronicities. Reiki helps us become clear channels of energy and light. Reiki allows us to become aware of and heal
the imbalances in ourselves and our lives. As we walk the
path of life one of our greatest challenges is to learn to view
the world with compassion, clarity, and without judgment.
Reiki calls us to be authentic, whole human beings filled
with integrity, love and light. As Reiki practitioners we
need to realize that every thought we have, and every
action we take impacts the entire planet. It is my belief that
consciousness vibrates in everything. A Reiki practitioner's
path includes learning to develop our own consciousness
through peacefulness, unconditional love, gratitude, compassion, and joy. This path is winding, curvy and filled with
rocks and challenges to overcome, but the mysteries that
unfold are the foundation of life.

A Basic Reiki Treatment

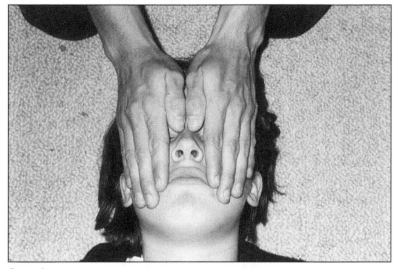

Step 1

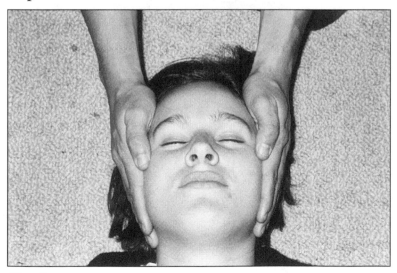

Step 2

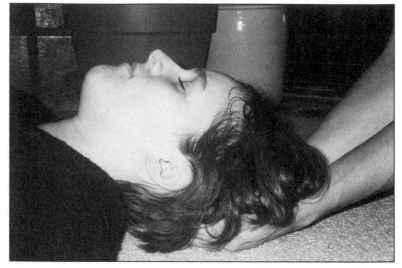

Step 3

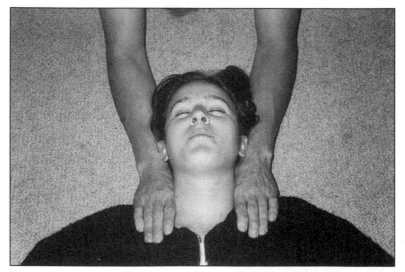

Step 4

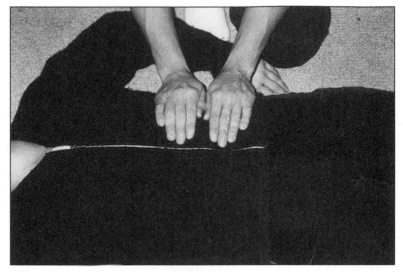

Step 5

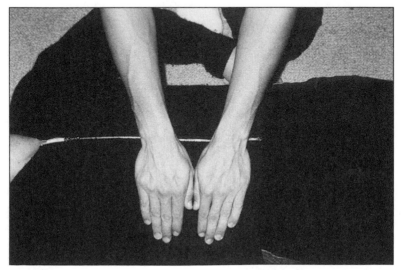

Step 6

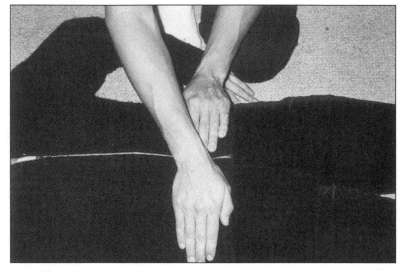

Step 7

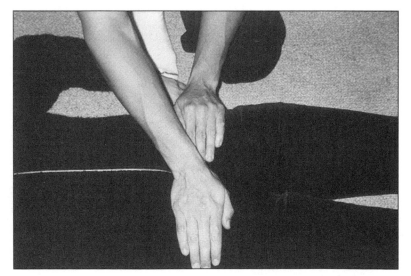

Step 8

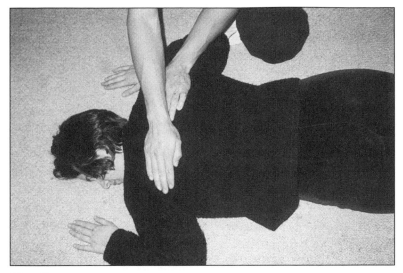

Step 9

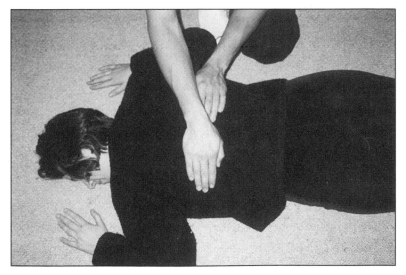

Step 10

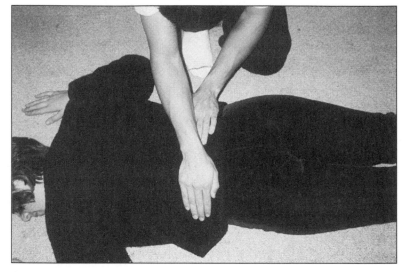

Step 11

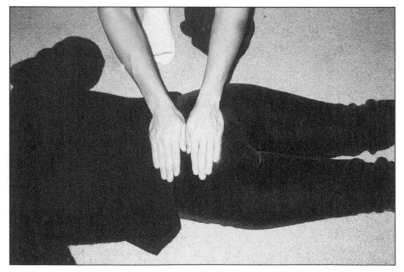

Step 12

Recommended Books

Arrien, Dr. Angeles. *The Four Fold Way*, Harper, San Francisco, 1993

Baginski, Bodo J. and Sharamon, Shalila. *Reiki, Universal Life Energy*, Life Rhythm, 1988

Bailey, Alice A. *The Consciousness of the Atom*, Lucis Publishing Co., 1922

Borchert, Bruno. *Mysticism*, Samuel Weiser, Inc., 1994

Brennan, Barbara Ann. *The Hands of Light*, Bantam Books, 1987

Capra, Fritjof. *The Web of Life*, Anchor Books, 1996

Casey, Karen. *Daily Meditations for Practicing The Course*, Harper, San Francisco, 1995

Chopra, Deepak. *Quantum Healing—Exploring the Frontiers of Mind/Body Medicine*, Bantam, 1989

Chopra, Deepak. *The Seven Spiritual Laws of Success*, Amber-Allen publishing, 1994

Chopra, Deepak. *Twenty Spiritual Lessons for Creating the Life You Want*, Harmony Books, 1995

Collinge, William. *Subtle Energy*, Warner Books, 1998

Combs, Allan and Holland, Mark. *Synchronicity, Science, Myth and the Trickster*, Marlowe & Company, 1996

A Course In Miracles, Foundation For Inner Peace, 1975

Cousineau, Phil. *Soul Moments*, Conari Press, 1997

Dossey, Dr. Larry. *Healing Words*, Harper, San Francisco, 1993

Doubleday, Tony and Scott, David. *The Elements of Zen*, Barnes & Noble Books, 1997

Ford, Arielle. *Hot Chocolate For The Mystical Soul*, Plume, 1998

Fox, Emmet. *Alter Your Life*, Harper & Row, 1931

Fox, Emmet. *Stake Your Claim*, Harper San Francisco, 1952

Fox, Matthew & Sheldrake, Rupert. *The Physics of Angels*, Harper San Francisco, 1996

Gerber, Dr. Richard. *Vibrational Medicine*, Bear & Company, 1988

Joy, Dr. W. Brugh. *Joy's Way*, J.P. Tarcher, Inc., 1979

Judith, Anodea. *Wheels of Life*, Llewellyn, 1987

Jung, Dr. Carl. *Synchronicity An Acausal Connecting Principle*, translated by R.F.C. Hull, Princeton University Press, 1969

Kornfield, Jack. *A Path with Heart*, Bantam Books, 1993

Linn, Denise. *The Secret Language of Signs*, Ballantine Books, 1996

Mansfield, Victor. *Synchronicity, Science and Soul-Making*, Open Court, 1995

Miller, Ronald S. & the Editors of New Age Journal, *As Above So Below*, 1992

Millman, Dan. *The Life You Were Born To Live*, H.J. Kramer, 1993

Millman, Dan. *The Laws of Spirit*, H.J. Kramer, 1995

Millman, Dan. *Everyday Enlightenment*, Warner Books, 1998

Myss, Dr. Caroline. *Anatomy of the Spirit*, Three River Press, 1996

Peat, F. David. *Synchronicity, the Bridge Between Matter and Mind*, Bantam Books, 1987

Progoff, Ira. *Jung, Synchronicity, and Human Destiny*, Dell Publishing Co., 1973

Redfield, James. *The Celestine Prophecy*, Warner Books, 1993

Redfield, James. *The Celestine Vision*, Warner Books, 1997

Rinpoche, Sogyal. *The Tibetan Book of Living and Dying*, Harper Collins, 1993

The Essential Rumi, Translated by Coleman Barks, Harper San Francisco, 1995.

Sui, Choa Kok. *Pranic Healing*, Samuel Weiser, Inc., 1990

St. Teresa of Avila. *Interior Castle*, Doubleday, 1961

Verschure, Yasmin. *Way To The Light*, Samuel Weiser, Inc., 1996

Weiss, Dr. Brian L. *Many Lives, Many Masters*, Warner Books, 1990

Weiss, Dr. Brian L. *Only Love Is Real*, Warner Books, Inc. 1996

Zukav, Gary. *The Seat of the Soul*, Simon & Schuster, Inc. 1989

Resources

International Society for the Study of
Subtle Energies and Energy Medicine
(ISSSEEM)
356 Goldco Circle
Golden, Colorado 80403
Website: http://www.nekesc.org/-issseem/

ISSSEEM is one of the leading organizations dedicated
to synthesizing traditional wisdom and healing arts with
scientific theory. ISSSEEM supports exploration of the
phenomena connected to energy healing such as reiki.

Health World Online
http://www.healthy.net

This is a wonderful resource on the internet. It is a com-
prehensive wellness and natural health site, with many
links to other sites.

Reiki Pages
http://www.angelfire.com

This is one of the better websites dedicated just to Reiki.

Healthfinder
http://www.healthfinder.org

This is a great site, especially for alternative health solutions and resources. Lists many conferences and workshops of a great variety.

Office of Alternative Medicine—OAM
National Institute of Health
http://www.altmed.od.nih.gov

This gives you a direct online connection to the office of alternative medicine. Many resources and links connected to this office.

Institute of Noetic Sciences
http://www.noetic.org
475 Gate Five Road, Suite 300
Sausalito, CA 94965

Edgar Mitchell, Apollo 14 astronaut founded this wonderful organization. It is a nonprofit organization that supports research and education on human potential, consciousness, transformation and other endeavors related to healing and subtle energy.

Omega Institute
http://www.omega-inst.org
260 Lake Drive
Rhinebeck, NY 12572

In 1977 Stephan Rechtchaffen founded the Omega Institute. It is the nation's largest and most progressive holistic learning center. They offer continuous workshops and classes throughout the year.

Association for Research and Enlightenment
http://www .are-cayce.com
P.O. Box 595
Virginia Beach, VA 23451-0595

This is a wonderful resource. A.R.E. was founded by Edgar Cayce years ago. They offer classes on a variety of health issues, metaphysics, etc.

Arts & Healing Network
http://www.artheals.org/
3450 Sacramento St. Box 612
San Francisco, CA 94118

This organization is dedicated to celebrating the connection between arts and healing. Their website serves as a international resource and exchange for anyone interested in the healing potential of art, especially environmentalists, social activists, artist, health care practitioners and those challenged by illness.

Creation Spirituality Network
http://www. csnet.org
2141 Broadway
Oakland, CA 94612-9944

This network is connected to Matthew Fox and his newsletter. It is a good resource for a variety of healing work that is going on around the country connected to Matthew Fox's center.

Have You Had a Mystical Experience You Would Like To Share?

If you have had a personal experience that was clearly connected to either Reiki or synchronicity, and you would like to share for a future volume please send it to:

Patricia Rose Upczak
Synchronicity Publishing
P.O. Box 927
Nederland, CO 80466
http://www.csd.net/~synchron

Please be sure to include your name, address and phone number.

Patricia Rose Upczak has worn many hats professionally over the last twenty years. She designed and developed the special education program for learning disabled students at a large high school in Boulder, Colorado in 1975. In 1985 she simultaneously became involved in writing and Reiki. She has been teaching Reiki classes for over nine years. Her first book, STEVE, a grieving process book for families, was published in early 1998. She is currently working on metaphysical mysteries for children.

For information about Patricia Rose Upczak's workshops and seminars please write or email your request to:

Patricia Rose Upczak
P.O. Box 927
Nederland, CO. 80466
email address: synchron@csd.net

Books from
Synchronicity Publishing

You may purchase Patricia Rose Upczak's books at your favorite bookstore, online at Amazon.com or at Synchronicity Publishing's website http://www.csd.net/~synchron, or fill out this order form , fax or mail it to us with your payment to:

Synchronicity Publishing
P.O. Box 927
Nederland, CO 80466
fax # 303-258-7917

To order copies of *Reiki, A Way of Life* ($13.99-ISBN# 1-891554-18-2), please fill out this form and return with your payment and $3.00 for shipping.

You may also order copies of *STEVE, a grieving process book for families* ($12.99-ISBN# 1-891554-15-8)
Death is an experience that we all must go through. Whether it be that of a parent, grandparent, friend, neighbor, child or ourselves. Some people deal with these experiences very young—others face this powerful, transformative ordeal later in life. The process however is the same for all of us. There is an old saying, " It doesn't matter what happens to you—it only matters how you deal with it." Many people grow and transform dramatically through their grieving over the death of a loved one. Some grow bitter and old beyond their years. As with all things we have a choice. This book is about those choices and decisions one family made.

Order Form

I wish to order:

_____ copies of _____ at $_____ each.

_____ copies of _____ at _____ each.

_____ copies of _____ at _____ each.

Book Total $_____

For shipping and handling, please add **$3.00**

Colorado residents please add

appropriate sale tax on total. $_____

Total $_____

Payment:

    ○ Check   ○ Money Order

    ○ Visa   ○ Mastercard

Account Number _____

Expiration Date _____

Please print exact name appearing on credit card:

_____

Signature _____

You may also fax your order if you are paying by credit card:
303-258-7917.

Thank you. We appreciate your business.